The Power of the Gospel

A Survey of Romans

The Power of the Gospel

A Survey of Romans

By

Dr. Steve Combs

Copyright © 2017 by *Steve Combs*

ISBN: 978-0-9985452-2-6

All rights reserved. No part of this publication may be reproduced or transmitted in any form or by any means, electronic or mechanical, including photocopy, recording, or any information storage and retrieval system, without permission from the copyright owner in writing.

The Author may be contacted by writing:
bpsg.scombs@gmail.org

This commentary is based on
the King James Bible

Published by:
The Old Paths Publications, Inc.
www.theoldpathspublications.com
TOP@theoldpathspublications.com

Table of Contents

Chapter		Page
	Introduction (Rom. 1:1-17)	7
1	The Condemnation of Mankind (Rom. 1:18-3:19)	16
2	The Justification of Believers (Rom. 3:20-5:21)	39
3	The Sanctification of Believers (Rom. 6:1-8:16)	60
4	The Glorification of Believers (Rom. 8:17-39)	97
5	The Confirmation of the Promises to Israel (Rom. 9:1-11:36)	113
6	The Dedication of the Believer's Life (Rom. 12:1-15:13)	155
7	Personal Notes and Conclusions (Rom. 15:14-16:27)	198
	Afterword: Election and Predestination	212
	About the Author	256
	End Notes	257

Introduction to the Book of Romans

Rom. 1:1-17

The Book of Romans was written about 58 A.D. by Paul, the apostle, to the Roman Church; it was probably written when he was in Corinth during his third missionary journey. [1] Rome was the largest city in the empire at the time, boasting a population of about 4 million. It is impossible to know for certain who started the church in Rome. It was not Paul, because he had never been there as a Christian. It was not likely that Peter started the church in Rome. Peter was in Jerusalem at the conference of Acts fifteen in 49 A.D. He was not there when Paul wrote Romans, because he would have been named among the greetings of Romans sixteen. The church was already a mature church when Paul wrote (Rom. 15:14). So, Peter probably did not start the church. A possibility is that one of Paul's converts started the church. Another possibility is that it was some of the Jews who were at Jerusalem on the day of Pentecost, when Peter preached and about 3000 were saved. Acts 2:10 says that among those listening to Peter's sermon were "strangers of Rome." [2] It could also have been Barnabas.

Paul was planning a trip to Rome (Rom. 1:10-11). He hoped to be able to minister to them and to obtain their support for traveling to Spain (Acts 15:24). The Book of Romans was written to them to perfect their understanding of salvation. It is the greatest book in the New Testament on that subject. The Book of Romans sets forth the great truths of sin, condemnation, propitiation, justification, reconciliation, propitiation, sanctification, and glorification. It presents the Lord Jesus Christ as the Son of David, the Son of God, the Savior of the world, and the hope of the Jews.

There are many ways to approach the Book of Romans. We shall divide the Book into six sections plus an introduction and a conclusion. Those sections will fall out as in Table 1 on the following page. This study is a survey. That is, we will take it paragraph-by-paragraph more often than verse-by-verse.

One final consideration remains before launching into the body of Romans. I have chosen to base this exposition on the King James Version of the Holy Bible. It is necessary to mention this, because there can be only one final authority when seeking the truth. Since there are textual issues that cause other versions to be in conflict with the KJV at various places and those conflicts are based on conflicting Greek texts (the UBS Text or the Received Text

How the Book of Romans is Organized

1:16-3:31	4:1-5:21	6:1-8:16	8:17-39
Condemnation	Justification	Sanctification	Glorification
Pain of wrath	Penalty of Sin	Power of Sin	Presence of Sin
No Salvation	Saved Spirit	Saved Soul	Saved Body
Price of Sin	Position	Practice	Predestination
Sinners	Savior	Saints	Secured
Without Righteousness	Declared Righteous	Made Godly	Growth Completed

9:1-11:36	12:1-15:7
Confirmation	Dedication
Preservation	Practical Walk
Saved Nation	Saved Walk
Promise	Purpose
Saved Jews	Standing Firm
A Great Nation	Glorifying God

Table 1

or the Majority Text), a decision must be made as to which English Version and which Greek text will be relied on as the truth and as the Word of God. An example of these differences is in Romans 8:1. The last half of the verse as it is in the KJV is missing in nearly all modern versions. After many years of study in manuscript evidence, Greek, English, and history, I am convinced that the KJV is the most accurate English Version available and the Received text it is based on is the correct Greek New Testament. I have never found an error in the KJV and I never expect to find one. Therefore, I accept the King James Version as the Word of God without error. For this reason, this exposition will be based on the wording of the KJV.

At times, illustrations and definitions may be drawn from the Greek Received Text, from which the KJV was translated. Some may actually object to this. I think, however, that their objection is based on the fact that many times references are made to the Greek and Hebrew texts for the purpose of attempting to prove the KJV is translated incorrectly. That is not what I do. I use those texts to confirm, defend, and explain the King James as it is translated.

Greeting and Address - Romans 1:1-8

Paul, a servant of Jesus Christ, called to be an apostle, separated unto the gospel of God, (Which he had promised afore by his prophets in the holy scriptures,) Concerning his Son Jesus Christ our Lord, which was made of the seed of David according to the flesh; And declared to be the Son of God with power, according to the spirit of holiness, by the resurrection from the dead: By whom we have received grace and apostleship, for obedience to the faith among all nations, for his name: Among whom are ye also the called of Jesus Christ: To all that be in Rome, beloved of God, called to be saints: Grace to you and peace from God our Father, and the Lord Jesus Christ. First, I thank my God through Jesus Christ for you all, that your faith is spoken of throughout the whole world.

Two persons and one group are identified and described in the epistle's greeting, Paul, the Lord Jesus Christ, and the saints in Rome. Paul is described as an apostle (one called and sent forth by Christ). He says his apostleship was by the will of God (2 Cor. 1:1), not of or by man (Gal. 1:1). He is "separated unto the gospel of God." That is, he was called to preach the gospel, the death burial and resurrection of Christ (1 Cor. 15:1-4). He was primarily sent to the Gentiles (Rom. 15:16-18), but according to his own statement in Romans 1:16, he had a ministry to the Jews. He said that God gave him grace and apostleship to bring people of all nations into obedience to Christ (Rom. 1:5). Paul made it clear that all he was and all he had accomplished was by the grace of God alone (Rom. 12:3; 1 Cor. 15:10), not in any way of himself (2 Cor. 3:5).

The gospel is all about the Lord Jesus Christ. The Lord is "the seed of David" according to human descent. But, He is also the "Son of God," a fact proved by His resurrection. Paul's apostleship and service were given by and received from the Lord Jesus. All service for Him is given and done by His grace alone. Without Him, we can do nothing (John 15:5), but with the strength of Christ, we can do all things (Phil. 4:13). We do not deserve a place of service; He gives it as He pleases. What a privilege it is to have a place of service for His glory!

The recipients of the letter, the Roman Christians, were "called to be saints" (Rom. 1:6-7). A "saint" is a person who has received initial sanctification, that is, they have been separated to God as His possession. When we place our faith in Jesus Christ, God chooses us to salvation and sanctifies us (2 Thess. 2:13-14). God picks us out of the masses of the world when we trust Christ and he makes us His own. He saves us from the penalty of sin. This is the beginning of the Christian life. It is the past of a Christian. As we live our lives, God leads us into a practical sanctification (1 Thess. 4:3-4), a process of separation from sin; growing and learning to live in obedience to Christ. This separation from the power of sin is the present life of a Christian. The future of a saint is bright with assurance and hope. In the future we will be conformed to the image of God's Son (Rom. 8:28-30). This will be the ultimate sanctification, when we are separated from the very presence of sin in us.

Paul's Desire to Travel to Rome Romans 1:9-17

For God is my witness, whom I serve with my spirit in the gospel of his Son, that without ceasing I make mention of you always in my prayers; Making request, if by any means now at length I might have a prosperous journey by the will of God to come unto you. For I long to see you, that I may impart unto you some spiritual gift, to the end ye may be established; That is, that I may be comforted together with you by the mutual faith both of you and me. Now I would not have you ignorant, brethren, that oftentimes I purposed to come unto you, (but was let hitherto,) that I might have some fruit among you also, even as among other Gentiles. I am debtor both to the Greeks, and to the Barbarians; both to the wise, and to the unwise. So, as much as in me is, I am ready to preach the gospel to you that are at Rome also. For I am not ashamed of the gospel of Christ: for it is the power of God unto salvation to every one that believeth; to the Jew first, and also to the Greek. For therein is the righteousness of God revealed from faith to faith: as it is written, The just shall live by faith.

Paul prayed for a "prosperous" journey to Rome (Rom. 1:9-13). God answered his prayer, but not like Paul hoped. His journey was prosperous and his stay in Rome was prosperous in a spiritual sense, but the trip and the accommodations were not as Paul would have liked. He wanted to prosper *them* by "imparting some spiritual gift" and "have some fruit among" them. However, he came to Rome as a prisoner several years after he wrote his letter to the Romans. Paul was arrested by the Romans in Jerusalem in Acts 23. He was in prison in Jerusalem a short while and transferred to Caesarea, where he was held for two years (Acts 24:27). When Paul appealed to Caesar, he was sent to Rome by the Roman Governor, Festus. On the way to Rome they endured shipwreck, but not before Paul was able to show Christian kindness to his captors and fellow-prisoners. All of them reached the shore of the island of Melita safe (Acts 27). There Paul was able to minister to some of the islanders (Acts 28:1-10). When Paul arrived in Rome, he was still a prisoner for at least two more years, but he was able to live in his own hired house and minister to the Jews and the Church (Acts 28:30-31). So, his journey and his stay in Rome were prosperous in a spiritual sense, but it was with difficulties and trouble.

Paul felt that He was under an obligation to preach the gospel (v. 14), so much so, that he felt himself to be in debt to the Jews and Gentiles. This feeling may have been because of his effort to destroy the church when he was unsaved (Gal. 1:23). Regardless, he knew he was called to preach the gospel and was separated to the gospel (Rom. 1:1; 1 Cor. 1:17). Paul was "ready" (v.15) to preach and he was "not ashamed" (v. 16) and he was confident in the "power" of the gospel (v.16). Part of the whole armor of the Christian is to be prepared to tell others about the gospel (Eph. 6:15). It is pictured as the shoes on our feet, indicating a readiness to go wherever God leads. The Bible says, "How beautiful are the feet of them that preach the gospel of peace, and bring glad tidings of good things!" (Rom. 10:15).

The gospel is defined as how "Christ died for our sins according to the scriptures; and that he was buried, and that he rose again the third day according to the scriptures" (1 Cor. 15:3-4). Its source is God's love and grace. Its effectiveness is by faith and the power of God (John 3:16; Eph. 2:8-9). Romans 1:16-17 are the key verses for the Book of Romans. The Book is all about the gospel and the life of faith. The gospel is the power of God to salvation for all. The Scripture says, "For the preaching of the cross is to them that perish foolishness; but unto us which are saved it is the power of God ... it pleased God by the foolishness of preaching to save them that believe" (1 Cor. 1:18, 21).

The cross makes a life of faith in the power of God possible. Without the cross there could be no life (see comments on chapter six). The Christian life is lived "by faith." It is not lived by self-effort or self-discipline. There is effort and discipline involved as part of the self-control necessary to live godly, but self–control and discipline (called "temperance") is a fruit of the Spirit (Gal. 5:22-24). It comes from the Faith that is produced in us by the Word of God (Rom. 10:17). So, we must have faith in all His truth, his promises, all His commands, and all other principles of living in the Word of God.

Chapter One

The Condemnation of Mankind
Romans 1:18-3:19

The first major point made in the Book of Romans is that "all have sinned" (Rom 3:23). It is a conclusion that summarizes this first large section. This point is approached from several standpoints. First, Romans 1:18-32 traces the path of descent taken by every nation starting with recognition of God and ending with failure, wickedness, and chaos. Second, Romans 2:1-29 proves that the Jews, as well as the Gentiles, are under sin and condemnation. Finally, Romans 3:1-31 shows the utter hopelessness of all mankind without Christ. The only hope is found in the redemption that is in Christ and justification by faith in Him.

The fall of the Nations (Rom. 1:18-32)

For the wrath of God is revealed from heaven against all ungodliness and unrighteousness of men, who hold the truth in unrighteousness (Rom. 1:18)

When we speak of nations here, the Bible is not looking at a *nation* the way it is understood in modern times. Today nations are defined the same way we define *countries*, as an organized geopolitical area of land. The Bible definition of nations centers on *groups of people*. The prime example is Israel, which was considered a nation before they conquered the land of Palestine (Ex. 33:13). Think of a nation in terms of the *Cherokee Nation* or the *Lakota Nation* or the *Arapaho Nation*. A Biblical nation is a group of people who, like Israel, have common ancestry, common language, and common laws or culture. These groups have similar ethnicity and language. They may be referred to as *ethno-linguistic* groups. Mission agencies often call them *people groups*. Every such group follows a similar downward path morally and spiritually. Each step downward is characterized by general rebellion of the group and, as a result, God gives them up to further descent. Today, every country has a general culture, but may have many of these ethno-linguistic groups. The downward steps can take place in that general culture as a whole and may affect multiple ethno-linguistic groups within the country.

Step One: Loss of Perspective Toward God

Because that which may be known of God is manifest in them; for God hath shewed it unto them. For the invisible things of him from the creation of the world are clearly seen, being understood by the things that are made, even his eternal power and Godhead; so that they are without excuse: Because that, when they knew God, they glorified

him not as God, neither were thankful; but became vain in their imaginations, and their foolish heart was darkened. Professing themselves to be wise, they became fools,
And changed the glory of the uncorruptible God into an image made like to corruptible man, and to birds, and fourfooted beasts, and creeping things.
(Rom. 1:18-23)

The first step downward is a loss of perspective in regard to God (Rom. 1:18-23). Biblically, cultural development started out, in Genesis 9 and 10, with a belief in one creator God. This is because God revealed Himself that way through creation and to Adam and Eve with His presence (vv. 18-20). Adam and Eve had this understanding after the expulsion from the Garden of Eden in Genesis 3 and they passed it on to their children. By the time of the Flood, about 2348 BC, the earth was full of violence of and great wickedness. After the Flood mankind was separated by the dividing of languages (Gen. 11). Each of the resulting ethno-linguistic groups started out with knowledge of the True God and His judgment of sin through the Flood. They fell from there. Many western countries, including Europe and the United States were mono-theistic at one time. Many of these cultures and countries have remained nominally mono-theistic, but they have all failed in two major ways: 1) They did not glorify God as God and 2) they quit recognizing their blessings as coming from God and being thankful to Him.

This earned them four terrible consequences:

1) They "became vain in their imaginations." An example of these imaginations is mankind's determination

to find explanations of the universe that do not include God, such as, evolution. While science taught that the earth was *not* the center of the universe, human beings began to imagine that they *are* the center of the universe and the pinnacle of all things. Instead of recognizing God as the Supreme sovereign of the universe, people began to imagine that they are highest all creatures. They began to see themselves as gods; "Ye shall be as gods," Satan has told them (Gen. 3:5).

2) These foolish imaginations came out of foolish hearts. Their foolish hearts "were darkened." They lost any understanding they could have had on the fundamental questions of life: who am I, where did I come from, who is God, what do I have to do with Him, and where am I going? This is certainly one of the reasons for the obsession of finding life on other planets. There is a desperate search for origins. The answers are in the Bible, but they will not believe the Bible.

3) "Professing themselves to be wise, they became fools" (V. 22). They were, therefore, self-deceived. The *International Standard Bible Encyclopedia* defines a fool as:

> The *fool* was he who was thoughtless, careless, conceited, self-sufficient, indifferent to God and His Will, or who might even oppose and scoff at religion and wise instruction ... the idea conveyed by which is that of one who is hasty, impatient, self-sufficient (Prov. 12:15; Prov. 15:5; 16:22); despising advice and instruction (Prov. 1:7; 14:9; 24:7); ready to speak and act without

thinking (Prov.10:14; 12:16; 20:3); quick to get angry, quarrel and cause strife (Prov. 11:29; 14:17 *'iwweleth*; 29:9); unrestrained in his anger (Job 5:2; Prov. 17:12); silly, stupid even with brute stupidity (Prov. 7:22; 26:11; 27:22; compare Is. 19:11; Jer.4:22); he is associated with "transgression" (Ps. 107:17; Prov. 13:15; 17:18, 19), with "sin" (Prov. 24:9), with the "scoffer" (same place) ; *'iwweleth*, "foolishness" occurs (Ps. 38:5; 69:5; Prov. 13:16; "folly," 14:8; 14:24; 14:29, etc.). [3]

4) They began to worship other gods (v. 23). In some cultures that was the worship of creatures, the sun, moon, or stars and in other cultures it was the worship of money, education, power, pleasure, self, etc.

In the U.S.A., this step took place from about 1875 to 1960. 1875 is about the time European religious liberalism came to the U.S. The early 1900's saw many battles between Bible believers and these liberals. 1950-60 is the approximate time Christian fundamentalists began to give up the fight against liberalism. During this time, the teaching of evolution gained control of the public schools. Finally, the Supreme Court removed prayer from the schools in 1962 and removed the Bible from the schools in 1963. The Beatles showed up in the United States in 1963. Whether they had anything to do with what it or not, the drug and sexual revolution followed on their heels.

Step Two: Given up to Sexual Corruption

Wherefore God also gave them up to uncleanness through the lusts of their own hearts, to dishonour their own bodies between themselves: Who changed the truth of God into a lie, and worshipped and served the creature more than the Creator, who is blessed for ever. Amen. (Rom. 1:24-25)

The second step is that God gave them up to sexual corruption (Rom. 1:24-25). The phrase "God ... gave them up" shows clearly that God restrains evil in a society. When God takes away that restraint, we sometimes say that "God is taking His hand off." The Scriptural phrase is "God gave them up to" whatever the next step downward happens to be.

In this case, God gave them up to "the lusts of their own hearts, to dishonor their own bodies between themselves" (v. 24). It involves "lust" and "bodies." Foolish hearts tend toward more and more sin. Fornication and adultery become a way of life. Pornography becomes open and eventually (in U.S. and European culture) enters the home and permeates lives through movies, magazines, books, television, computers, internet, and cell phones. Romans 1:25 makes it clear that this sexual obsession is actually worship. By doing these things they "worshipped and served the creature more than the Creator." According to Colossians 3:5 this lust is a type of worship, because it is "covetousness, which is idolatry."

It is also said that they changed the "truth of God into a lie." God created sex and it was mentioned in Genesis 1 and 2. Sex was created as a joyful relationship between husband and wife (Prov. 5:15-20). Through the sexual relationship husband and wife are made "one flesh" (Gen. 3:24). It is the cement that locks two people together in the creation of a new family. Now sex is seen as merely a means of intense pleasure and reproduction. Many have been convinced that God's truth and plan about sex is a lie. They are convinced they are missing out on something good by not having sex outside marriage, just as Eve fell for the same lie when the devil convinced her she was missing out by not eating the fruit of the forbidden tree.

The United States experienced this during the "sexual revolution." The removal of the Bible and prayer from schools was probably the final watershed acts that caused God to give up our culture to sexual corruption. The back ground and preparation for this movement took place in the late 1950's with the playboy movement. The main revolution broke loose in the 1960's and 1970's. God took His hand off us again.

Step Three: Vile Affections (Rom. 1:26-27)

For this cause God gave them up unto vile affections: for even their women did change the natural use into that which is against nature: And likewise also the men, leaving the natural use of the woman, burned in their lust one toward another; men with men working that which is unseemly, and receiving in themselves that recompence of their error which was meet.

The third downward step is when "God gave them up unto vile affections" (Rom. 1:26-27). What are

these vile affections? It is a behavior described as:
1) The "women did change the natural use into that which is against nature" (v.26) and
2) the "men, leaving the natural use of the woman, burned in their lust one toward another" (v.27); men lusting for men, and
3) there were "men with men working that which is unseemly" (v. 27). "Unseemly" means indecent; men being indecent with men.

Men lusting for men, women performing acts which are against nature, men doing indecent things with other men are characteristics that can only be homosexuality and possibility bestiality. Male homosexuality in the U. S. is called "gay," a word that used to mean, "Merry; airy; jovial; sportive; frolicksome." It denotes more life and animation than cheerful." [4] The homosexual lifestyle is anything but *gay* in that sense. In the Bible a male homosexual is called "effeminate" and an "abuser" of himself "with mankind" (1 Cor. 6:9).

Here, in Romans 1, God speaks of Homosexuality as being indecent, vile affections, and against nature. The Bible shows clearly that God is against homosexuality. There are some people who teach against homosexuality and homosexual marriage by focusing on *natural law*. God has placed a conscience in mankind. Both that conscience and the Scriptures testify that homosexuality is sin. In Genesis 1, God made man. In fact, "male and female created he them" (Gen. 1:29). Why did God make a male and a female? Why did He not make two males? In Genesis 2:18, God said, "It is not good that the man should be alone; I will make him an help meet for him." Then God proceeded to make a woman and brought her to Adam, who named her "Eve" and called her *wife*. Why was the first wife a woman and not another man? Man needed a companion and a helper fit for him. God gave him a woman to fulfill those needs. Another man would not be able to meet those needs. Men and women need compliments to themselves, not another of the same. God is the God who created nature. Nature's God made it natural that only a male and a female compliment and fulfill the needs of the other. Same sex relationships were not designed by the God of nature to provide that fulfillment. Therefore, same sex relationships or marriages are a perversion of God's natural design. They are "against nature."

In 2016, the Supreme Court of the United States issued a decision that made homosexual marriage legal throughout the entire country. However, homosexual liaisons are *not marriage* in a natural or Biblical sense. When God brought Eve to Adam the formula for marriage is conveyed as, "Therefore shall a man leave his father and his mother, and shall cleave unto his wife: and they shall be one flesh" (Gen. 2:24). This verse gives a three-fold formula that creates a marriage: 1) leave father and mother, 2) cleave to your wife, 3) become one flesh. This obviously implies a public commitment. To leave one's parents and make a total commitment (cleave) to one's wife will be a public event. The Bible does not prescribe a specific marriage ceremony, but the breaking of an old relationship and establishing a new one will certainly be made publicly known in some way.

Homosexual relationship could qualify under the first part of the formula, but they cannot Biblical qualify under the second, because the Bible defines "wife" as a woman and "husband" as a man. Homosexual relationships can never qualify under the third part, either biblically or naturally. Homosexual partners can never become "one flesh." The one flesh relationship is defined in the Bible as a sexual relationship (1 Cor. 6:16). Men and women are physically designed by nature's God to interact sexually. Two males or two women are not. They may touch their bodies together, but this is *not* a one flesh relationship. Since, husband and wife are said to be ONE flesh, the sexual relationship is designed to create a bond between two people that literally creates a new thing – a new family. This occurs by bonding two people into an almost in-severable relationship and by producing children. Children cannot be naturally produced in a homosexual relationship.

These verses speak of both male and female homosexuals, but particularly of male homosexuals as "receiving in themselves that recompense of their error which was meet (fitting)" (v. 27). The homosexual movement in the U. S. gained open notoriety in the 1980's. Along with the "gay" movement another overwhelming disaster arose: AIDS, a deadly disease particularly associated with male homosexual behavior. AIDS was one of the unfortunate recompenses received *"in themselves"* by those in this lifestyle and others with whom they had sexual relations (if they were bi-sexual).

Step Four: A Reprobate Mind

And even as they did not like to retain God in their knowledge, God gave them over to a reprobate mind, to do

those things which are not convenient; Being filled with all unrighteousness, fornication, wickedness, covetousness, maliciousness; full of envy, murder, debate, deceit, malignity; whisperers, Backbiters, haters of God, despiteful, proud, boasters, inventors of evil things, disobedient to parents, Without understanding, covenant breakers, without natural affection, implacable, unmerciful: Who knowing the judgment of God, that they which commit such things are worthy of death, not only do the same, but have pleasure in them that do them.
(Rom. 1:28-32)

The fourth and final step is a reprobate mind and its results (Rom. 1:28-32). By this time, a society comes to the point where it tries to erase all knowledge of God. They do not want God to be mentioned. They do not want His will to be discussed or to be acknowledged. Because of this, God lets their minds become reprobate. The word "reprobate" means "That which is rejected on account of its own worthlessness (Jer. 6:30; Heb. 6:8; Gr. *adokimos*, "rejected")." [5] The reprobate mind is a mind that is so bad that it must be disapproved and rejected by God.

What kind of mind is that? It must be a godless mind, because it rejects all knowledge of God. It refuses to acknowledge Him in any way. It must be a carnal mind in the extreme. The Bible says that the carnal mind is the enemy of God (Rom. 8:6-7). It would be a mind hardened in pride against God (Dan. 5:20). It is a mind that has rejected God and His law. Therefore, it is a mind that finds it very difficult to discern between moral right and wrong and between good, better, and best.

The government of the USA has totally embraced and approved of homosexuality. *Is it any wonder many government leaders think the way they do? Is it any wonder there seems to be such a lack of common sense?*

The reprobate mind leads them "to do those things which are not convenient" (v. 28). This is followed in verses 29-31 by a list of the wicked sinful practices and attitudes that are not convenient. It ends with the statement, "Who knowing the judgment of God, that they which commit such things are worthy of death, not only do the same, but have pleasure in them that do them" (v. 32). These are all results of the reprobate mind. Mankind becomes "filled" with these things.

This entire process, starting with a failure to glorify God, leads to the worst possible cultural and societal conditions. The United States is currently, from 2000 A.D. forward, rejecting the knowledge of God, because as a culture it has accepted homosexuality. If it seems that the leaders of the United States and the western world do not have sense enough to take an umbrella into a rain storm, the reason is most likely too many reprobate minds.

Moral conditions in the USA in 2016 were evaluated by Armstrong Williams, the Business Manager of Ben Carson, brain surgeon and former presidential candidate:

> As a conservative, I have long decried the moral decline in America – from the sexually debasing rap music lyrics, to the declining significance of marriage and monogamy, to the virtual banishment of the word 'God' from the public sphere. We live in an age in which the top-selling

novel among women is a book called Fifty-Shades of Grey, a novel that flirts with sexual taboos in the nether-world between sex, violence, rape and consent. The implication being of course that there are fifty shades of damnation to which the human soul can fall prey. **Blacks use the n-word with so much frequency in pop music that it has become a central feature, a fact that is ultimately confusing to white listeners who are encouraged to listen to the music, and yet strictly forbidden from repeating the n-word contained in almost every other line of the lyrics.** Even I, who used to cringe every time I heard the word, have grown somewhat immune to the coarsening of public language and degradation of culture that has eroded our values. [6]

Although Mr. William's evaluation is mild in comparison to the true moral condition in America, he captures much of the fallen spirit in the country. This is not, by any means, limited to America. For example, I traveled to Thailand in May 2016. While there, I was told that the homosexual movement was very strong in the country. The king's son, it was said, was dying from Aids. I have used the United States as an example of these things. However, sin is universal and the steps downward to moral destruction are also universal. They apply to every nation. The movement downward may take a long time, but it is certain for those who turn from God. A nation may experience revival that stops the downward trend for a time, but the carnal heart of man is always in danger of turning away from God again.

The Righteous Judgment of God (Rom. 2:1-29)

1 Therefore thou art inexcusable, O man, whosoever thou art that judgest: for wherein thou judgest another, thou condemnest thyself; for thou that judgest doest the same things.
2 But we are sure that the judgment of God is according to truth against them which commit such things.
3 And thinkest thou this, O man, that judgest them which do such things, and doest the same, that thou shalt escape the judgment of God?
4 Or despisest thou the riches of his goodness and forbearance and longsuffering; not knowing that the goodness of God leadeth thee to repentance?
5 But after thy hardness and impenitent heart treasurest up unto thyself wrath against the day of wrath and revelation of the righteous judgment of God;
6 Who will render to every man according to his deeds:
7 To them who by patient continuance in well doing seek for glory and honour and immortality, eternal life:
8 But unto them that are contentious, and do not obey the truth, but obey unrighteousness, indignation and wrath,
9 Tribulation and anguish, upon every soul of man that doeth evil, of the Jew first, and also of the Gentile;
10 But glory, honour, and peace, to every man that worketh good, to the Jew first, and also to the Gentile:
11 For there is no respect of persons with God.
12 For as many as have sinned without law shall also perish without law: and as many as have sinned in the law shall be judged by the law;

13 (For not the hearers of the law are just before God, but the doers of the law shall be justified.
14 For when the Gentiles, which have not the law, do by nature the things contained in the law, these, having not the law, are a law unto themselves:
15 Which shew the work of the law written in their hearts, their conscience also bearing witness, and their thoughts the mean while accusing or else excusing one another;)
16 In the day when God shall judge the secrets of men by Jesus Christ according to my gospel.

The scathing condemnation of chapter one is followed by bringing mankind face to face with the judgment of God. God, in His judgment, operates on a set list of *foundational principles*:

1) His judgment is *according to truth* (v. 2).

2) God judges everyone *according to their own personal deeds, good or bad* (6).

3) Those who do well *are rewarded with eternal life* (v. 7, 10).

4) Those who obey unrighteousness *are rewarded with indignation and wrath* (v. 8, 9).

5) God's judgment is the same for everyone because *there is no respect of persons with God* (v. 11). God does not play favorites in matters of judgment.

6) Those who know the Law of Moses *will be judged by the law* (v. 12).

7) Those who do not know the Law of Moses have a conscience that tells them right and wrong, good and bad. They *will be judged without the Law* (vv. 12, 14).

8) Finally, *no one will escape God's judgment* (v. 3).

If any of this sounds like salvation by works, be patient. The Book of Romans is only dealing with sin, judgment, and condemnation up to this point. Judgment falls because of failure to keep God's law, whether it is the written law or the law in your heart. After Christ paid for our sins by shedding His blood on the cross, condemnation falls not only for that reason, but also because of unbelief in Him (John 3:18-20). However, nothing has been said about the grace of God in Jesus Christ since chapter one verses 16 and 17. The basic rule is that if you are good and perfect in your righteousness and in keeping the law, you will be rewarded with eternal life. If you do not do these things, you will face God's wrath and condemnation. That is the clear teaching of Romans 2:6-11. However, who is obedient and righteous like that and always exhibits the right attitude? No one is, because of our fallen nature. That is what we will learn in chapter three and that is why Jesus had to die on the cross and that is why salvation cannot come by works. We just aren't to that point in Romans, yet.

Chapter two starts out explaining why it is unwise to judge and condemn others (1-6). All that is accomplished by those who do this is that they condemn themselves. They also are guilty of breaking the law of God. God is very harsh on those who have this attitude. Do you think you will escape the judgment of God? Do you despise God's goodness, which leads you to repentance? The person who judges others exhibits a hard and unrepentant heart. Those who are judgmental toward others generally ignore God's judgment on themselves and do not realize that He loves them and wishes them to repent (v.4).

> 17 Behold, thou art called a Jew, and restest in the law, and makest thy boast of God,
> 18 And knowest his will, and approvest the things that are more excellent, being instructed out of the law;
> 19 And art confident that thou thyself art a guide of the blind, a light of them which are in darkness,
> 20 An instructor of the foolish, a teacher of babes, which hast the form of knowledge and of the truth in the law.
> 21 Thou therefore which teachest another, teachest thou not thyself? thou that preachest a man should not steal, dost thou steal?
> 22 Thou that sayest a man should not commit adultery, dost thou commit adultery? thou that abhorrest idols, dost thou commit sacrilege?
> 23 Thou that makest thy boast of the law, through breaking the law dishonourest thou God?
> 24 For the name of God is blasphemed among the Gentiles through you, as it is written.

When we arrive at verse 17, it becomes clear that God is including the Jews and that it is the Jews in particular who are judging others, especially the gentiles. Romans 2:17-24 gives a clear picture of the self-righteous attitudes of the Jews. Their special place as God's chosen earthly people gave them an unwarranted pride. They boasted of the fact that God gave them the law, not realizing that the law was given as a schoolmaster to bring us to Christ (Gal.

3:24-25). They boasted of knowing God's will and being instructed out of the law. They were confident that they were qualified to be teachers of the blind, the foolish, and of spiritual babies. However, though they were proud and boasted in the law, they did not keep the law. They condemned others for not keeping the law. They looked down on the Gentiles for not having the law and for not being a part of the covenants Israel had with God. Unfortunately, they brought dishonor to God, because of their failures to obey the law (v. 24).

> *25 For circumcision verily profiteth, if thou keep the law: but if thou be a breaker of the law, thy circumcision is made uncircumcision.*
> *26 Therefore if the uncircumcision keep the righteousness of the law, shall not his uncircumcision be counted for circumcision?*
> *27 And shall not uncircumcision which is by nature, if it fulfil the law, judge thee, who by the letter and circumcision dost transgress the law?*
> *28 For he is not a Jew, which is one outwardly; neither is that circumcision, which is outward in the flesh:*
> *29 But he is a Jew, which is one inwardly; and circumcision is that of the heart, in the spirit, and not in the letter; whose praise is not of men, but of God.*

On the other hand, the Gentiles had some advantages. The Jews were confident in their covenant relationship with God. This was because of their circumcision which was a token of the covenant between God and Israel (Gen. 17:11). Gentiles did not have that sign. However, disobedience to the law nullified a Jew's circumcision and when a Gentile kept the righteousness of the law, it counted to him as circumcision (vv. 25-26). Therefore, the Gentile, who seeks to obey God according to the dictates of his conscience, condemns the Jew for his transgressions (v. 27). The basic thought is that a real covenant relationship with God is found in the heart of an individual, not in outward rituals like circumcision.

These are God's basic standards of judgment. The major question each of us should ask is how will I fare in "the day when God shall judge the secrets of men by Jesus Christ" (Rom. 2:16)? The fact is that the Jew has failed to keep the written law and the Gentile has failed to follow the law of his conscience. Chapter three will tell us that if we face the judgment of God alone, none of us will fare well. Condemnation is all that awaits us, because we all fall short of the requirement of doing well in verses seven and ten.
None of us keeps the law. We cannot stand alone. We need some serious help and that (as we shall see) only comes from the Lord Jesus Christ.

The Entire World - Guilty before God
(Rom. 3:1-20)

1 What advantage then hath the Jew? or what profit is there of circumcision?
2 Much every way: chiefly, because that unto them were committed the oracles of God.
3 For what if some did not believe? shall their unbelief make

the faith of God without effect?
4 God forbid: yea, let God be true, but every man a liar; as it is written, That thou mightest be justified in thy sayings, and mightest overcome when thou art judged.
5 But if our unrighteousness commend the righteousness of God, what shall we say? Is God unrighteous who taketh vengeance? (I speak as a man)
6 God forbid: for then how shall God judge the world?
7 For if the truth of God hath more abounded through my lie unto his glory; why yet am I also judged as a sinner?
8 And not rather, (as we be slanderously reported, and as some affirm that we say,) Let us do evil, that good may come? whose damnation is just.

If the Jew is a law breaker the same as a Gentile, what is the advantage of being a Jew and of circumcision? They have many advantages, such as, the priesthood, special promises, a position as God's chosen nation, knowledge of who God is, and so on. The main advantage is that they were given the Scriptures, the Word of God. The Gentiles did not have that privilege. Jesus explained the reason why it is an advantage to have the Scriptures, "Search the scriptures; for in them ye think ye have eternal life: and they are they which testify of me" (John 5:39). He further said, "If ye continue in my word, then are ye my disciples indeed; and ye shall know the truth, and the truth shall make you free." (John 8:31-32). "Sanctify them through thy truth: thy word is truth" (John 17:17). God stated something similar in Matthew 4:4, "Man shall not live by bread alone, but by every word that proceedeth out of the mouth of God." How, pray tell, can you know the truth if you have never read or studied the Scriptures? You may learn from sermons, but no preacher can preach often enough to speak to all the needs of a moderate size congregation. More is needed. Each Christian must learn to feed himself on the Word of God.

This brings up an important topic. If the Scriptures are so necessary to the life of a Christian, shouldn't we do everything we can to make sure the Bible is available in every language? There are over 7,000 languages on earth. Only about 530 languages have the whole Bible and another 1300 or so have the New Testament. Nearly 4,000 languages have nothing of the Word of God, as far as is known. [7] True, some of those languages only have a few speakers; maybe 500 or so. Nevertheless, their souls are as important as mine and if I was them, I would want the Word of God in my language. This is a necessary task. The Great Commission (Mt. 28:19-20) cannot be fulfilled without Bible translation work.

Not all the Jews believed the Scriptures God gave them (v. 3). Nevertheless, God is true no matter what anyone thinks. God is right no matter what objection is brought against His truth and judgment, He will still prevail. In the vernacular, God calls the shots and the shots He calls are always right (vv. 3-8). Even if the unrighteousness of man makes God's righteousness appear as it is, glorious and holy, that still does not excuse the unrighteousness of man. God is true and right in all His judgments. Verse 4 indicates that men challenge God's truth and they will probably do this at the Great White Throne Judgment (Rev.20:11-15). Nevertheless, God's Word is always found to be true and everyone who speaks contrary to His Word is a liar.

9 What then? are we better than they? No, in no wise: for we have before proved both Jews and Gentiles, that they are all under sin;
10 As it is written, There is none righteous, no, not one:
11 There is none that understandeth, there is none that seeketh after God.
12 They are all gone out of the way, they are together become unprofitable; there is none that doeth good, no, not one.
13 Their throat is an open sepulchre; with their tongues they have used deceit; the poison of asps is under their lips:
14 Whose mouth is full of cursing and bitterness:
15 Their feet are swift to shed blood:
16 Destruction and misery are in their ways:
17 And the way of peace have they not known:
18 There is no fear of God before their eyes.
19 ¶Now we know that what things soever the law saith, it saith to them who are under the law: that every mouth may be stopped, and all the world may become guilty before God.
20 Therefore by the deeds of the law there shall no flesh be justified in his sight: for by the law is the knowledge of sin.

These next eleven verses (9-19) level one of the most scorching condemnations of mankind to ever be written. It is mankind in general that is in view. When one looks at the whole of the human race and sees these activities, it is a sad and dark picture. Every individual is not guilty of every sinful *activity*, but all the activities are prevalent in the human race. These sinful practices are not just present in the human race, they are the outstanding characteristics of the race. They are the spiritual condition of mankind. We are all participants. We are all guilty.

However, there are certain characteristics mentioned that seem to be universal. They are connected with the word "none." No one is *righteous.* Therefore, no one qualifies for eternal life under the rules of Romans 2. No one *understands* spiritual truth. Therefore, the Holy Spirit must convince the world of sin, righteousness, and judgment (John 16:7-11). The Holy Spirit must open our understanding (Lk. 24:45; John 16:12-14) and teach "all truth." None do *good,* because our good deeds compared to God's total goodness are nothing but filthy rags (Is. 64:6). Therefore, we have all become *unprofitable.* What a bleak picture!

All of it is to prove one point: that "both Jews and Gentiles ... are all under sin" (v. 9). All of us have failed to keep the Law and all of us are guilty before God (v. 19). We might as well forget about doing well, spoken about in chapter two. None of us can ever do well enough to earn eternal life. We are failures, bound for God's judgment and condemnation. This is why no flesh can be righteous by keeping the Law (v. 20). We are unable to keep the Law. God's righteous standards are beyond the ability of fallen human beings.

Chapter Two

The Justification of Believers
Romans 3:20-5:21

Thank God, He did not leave us in such a condition. God is a God of justice. Therefore, He must punish sin. He could justly and righteously punish all mankind and put us all in Hell. However, God is also a God of compassion and mercy. The Bible says God is love (1 John 4:8, 16). Therefore, God has an answer for the sin problem. That answer is in His Son, Jesus Christ (John 3:16; Rom. 3:22-24). God's provision for us is found in our redemption and justification through the blood Christ shed on the cross and by Christ's resurrection (Rom. 3:21-31). It is explained and exemplified by the justification of Abraham by faith (Rom. 4). It is made a reality in our reconciliation to God (Rom. 5).

God's Answer to the Sin Problem
Romans 3:21-31

21 But now the righteousness of God without the law is manifested, being witnessed by the law and the prophets;
22 Even the righteousness of God which is by faith of Jesus Christ unto all and upon all them that believe: for there is no difference:
23 For all have sinned, and come short of the glory of God;
24 Being justified freely by his grace through the redemption that is in Christ Jesus:
25 Whom God hath set forth to be a propitiation through faith in his blood, to declare his righteousness for the remission of sins that are past, through the forbearance of God;
26 To declare, I say, at this time his righteousness: that he might be just, and the justifier of him which believeth in Jesus.

God's answer to the sin problem as revealed in Romans 3 can be condensed into four words: justification (Rom. 3:21-24), redemption (Rom. 3:24), propitiation (Rom. 3:25-26), and remission (Rom. 3:25). This is salvation from the penalty of our sins and it is free. It comes to us only by God's grace through faith, not by good works (Rom. 3:27-28; also see Eph. 2:8-9). It is not limited or restricted to the Jews. Gentiles are as freely accepted as Jews (Rom. 3:29-30).

"*For all have sinned, and come short of the glory of God; being **justified** freely by his grace through the redemption that is in Christ Jesus*" (Rom. 3:23-24).

Justification is "a just acquittal from guilt" [8] and "an act of free grace by which God pardons the sinner and accepts him as righteous, on account of the atonement of Christ." [9] Justification is when "God imputeth righteousness without works" (Rom. 4:6). "Impute" means, "To reckon to one what does not belong to him." [10] The Scripture also says, "Blessed is the man to whom the Lord will not impute sin" (Rom. 4:7). Then on one hand, God reckons or counts righteousness to a person and, on the other hand, God refuses to count that person, whom He has justified, as a guilty sinner. When He justifies a person, God considers him to be righteous. This passage (Rom. 3:1-24) reveals several characteristics of justification:

1) It is called "the righteousness of God without the Law" (v. 21).
2) It is called "the righteousness of God which is by faith of Jesus Christ" (v. 22).
3) It is upon all who believe, because all have sinned (vv. 22-23).
4) So, it is by faith (v. 22).
5) It is free (v. 24).
6) It is by grace (v. 24). It is not of the Law and it is not of works. It is only through faith.
7) It is found only in Jesus Christ (v. 22, 24).

Verse 24 also says that justification is "through the *redemption* that is in Christ Jesus." Redemption is "a releasing, for (i.e., on payment of) a ransom." [11] It is a payment made for our freedom. Ephesians 2:1-3 says we are under the domination of the world, the devil, and our own flesh. The redemption price purchased our freedom from this domination. God bought us and we now belong to

Him (1 Cor. 6:19-20). The price that was paid was the precious blood of Christ (1 Peter 1:18-19) and it was paid to God. "None of them can by any means redeem his brother, nor give to God a ransom for him" (Ps. 49:7). None could redeem mankind by paying the ransom, except Jesus Christ, the perfect unblemished Lamb of God (Lev. 1:10; John 1:29, 36). The redemption is in Christ (v. 24) and our faith is in His blood (v. 25).

God's answer to man's sin problem also involves *propitiation*. This word is only used three times in Scripture. In 1 John 2:2 and 4:10, Christ, the Son of God, is said to be our propitiation. "Whom God hath set forth to be a propitiation through faith in his blood" (Rom. 3:25). The Greek word used in Romans 3:25 is translated "mercy seat" in Hebrews 9:5. The *mercy seat* was the lid of the Ark of the Covenant. In the Old Testament, on the Day of Atonement, the high priest went into the Holy of Holies in the Tabernacle (later the Temple) to offer the blood of the sacrifice made to atone for the sins of the people. This blood was presented to God before the mercy seat (Lev. 23:27-32; Heb. 9:7). Romans 1:18 says, "For the wrath of God is revealed from heaven against all ungodliness and unrighteousness of men." The propitiation is that which satisfies or appeases God's wrath. [12] [13] What is it that satisfied God's wrath and obtained His mercy? It is the blood Christ shed on the cross, "Whom God hath set forth to be a propitiation through faith in his blood" (v. 25). God's sense of justice required that sin be punished. The Lord Jesus Christ was sent to be the One who was punished for our sins (Romans 5:8; John 3:16). He, in His death, became the satisfaction or propitiation of God's wrath against sin and disobedience. God must be able to justify men, yet remain just Himself. The only way to do that was to allow someone to take the punishment for sin, to satisfy the just requirements against sin; then and only then could God offer mercy to the sinner (v. 26).

Finally, the propitiation and the payment of the redemption price leads to *remission* of our sins. Remission means to pass over something or to let it go. [14] When Jesus offered the fruit of the vine to His disciples at the last supper, He declared, "For this is my blood of the new testament, which is shed for many for the remission of sins" (Mt. 26:28). The remission of sins equals the forgiveness of sins. Eph. 1:7 puts it this way: "In whom we have redemption through his blood, the forgiveness of sins, according to the riches of his grace."

All of this provides us with an understanding of the nature of *grace.* We may infer that *grace* is God's rich mercy bestowed upon an undeserving and guilty sinner, whereby God himself pays for the sinner's sins through the blood of His Son, Jesus Christ, and grants the sinner redemption, justification, and forgiveness of all sin, past and future. What a wonderful Savior and God!

> *27 Where is boasting then? It is excluded. By what law? of works? Nay: but by the law of faith. 28 Therefore we conclude that a man is justified by faith without the deeds of the law.*

These verses place a strong emphasis on one of the most important points of the salvation God offers us. Salvation is all by grace, God's undeserved mercy, through faith without good works (Titus 3:5). This will also be emphasized in chapter four. The fact is that no one can be good enough or do enough good things to earn his way to heaven. If you could keep the standard of righteousness explained in Romans 2, perfect obedience to the law, you might earn your way to Heaven. However, that would make you as good as God. You cannot reach that standard. There are two basic reasons for this: 1) our fleshy nature is sinful and makes it impossible to do and 2) we all have sinned, we are sinners, and we must face the penalty for our sins no matter how much good we do otherwise. Finally, salvation is all to the glory of God and nothing goes to man's glory. There is nothing a person can do to save himself and, therefore, he cannot boast (v. 27; Eph. 2:8-9).

> *30 Seeing it is one God, which shall justify the circumcision by faith, and uncircumcision through faith.*
> *31 Do we then make void the law through faith? God forbid: yea, we establish the law.*

Chapter three ends by restating that God is the God of both the Jews and Gentiles (vv. 29-30). It then declares that the principle of salvation through and by faith establishes the law. How is this so? Galatians has the answer:

> *But the scripture hath concluded all under sin, that the promise by faith of Jesus Christ might be given to them that believe. But before faith came, we were kept under the law, shut up unto*

> the faith which should afterwards be revealed. Wherefore the law was our schoolmaster to bring us unto Christ, that we might be justified by faith. But after that faith is come, we are no longer under a schoolmaster. For ye are all the children of God by faith in Christ Jesus.(Gal. 3:22-26)

The Law, as a schoolmaster, teaches us that we have come short of God's standard of righteousness. It shows us that regardless of how hard we try, we continue to fall short. It brings us to the conclusion that our situation is hopeless. The purpose of the Law is to cause us to run to Christ as our only hope of salvation.

Abraham-Our Example and Explanation of Justification (Romans 4:1-25)

Romans 4:1-8 introduces us to an incident that took place in the life of Abraham. It comes from Genesis 15:1-6 and goes like this:

> After these things the word of the LORD came unto Abram in a vision, saying, Fear not, Abram: I am thy shield, and thy exceeding great reward. And Abram said, Lord GOD, what wilt thou give me, seeing I go childless, and the steward of my house is this Eliezer of Damascus? And Abram said, Behold, to me thou hast given no seed: and, lo, one born in my house is mine heir. And, behold, the word of the LORD

> *came unto him, saying, This shall not be thine heir; but he that shall come forth out of thine own bowels shall be thine heir. And he brought him forth abroad, and said, Look now toward heaven, and tell the stars, if thou be able to number them: and he said unto him, So shall thy seed be. And he believed in the LORD; and he counted it to him for righteousness.*

Abraham (then known as Abram) was old and he was worried. He had no children. Therefore, he had no heir except the steward of his house, Eliezer of Damascus. Though Eliezer was born among Abraham's family and servants, he was not Abraham's son. Abraham brought his complaint to God in prayer, as we all should do. God's answer was two-fold: Abraham would have a child who would be his heir and, when he had looked at the stars as God instructed him, he was told that his descendants would be as numerous as were the stars. Genesis 15:6 says, "And he believed in the LORD; and he counted it to him for righteousness." *This is the definition of justification.*

This all took place before God gave the Law to Moses. It is evident from the example that good works and Law keeping have nothing to do with justification. As Romans 4:1-8 says:

> 1 What shall we say then that Abraham our father, as pertaining to the flesh, hath found?
> 2 For if Abraham were justified by works, he hath whereof to glory; but not before God.
> 3 For what saith the scripture? Abraham

> believed God, and it was counted unto him for righteousness.
> 4 Now to him that worketh is the reward not reckoned of grace, but of debt.
> 5 But to him that worketh not, but believeth on him that justifieth the ungodly, his faith is counted for righteousness.
> 6 Even as David also describeth the blessedness of the man, unto whom God imputeth righteousness without works,
> 7 Saying, Blessed are they whose iniquities are forgiven, and whose sins are covered.
> 8 Blessed is the man to whom the Lord will not impute sin.

Abraham did not get justified before God by works. It was totally by faith. Had it been in any way of works, justification would have been given in payment of a debt God owed Abraham. On the contrary, justification was (and is) a free gift. God doesn't owe it to us. He gives it by grace.

Circumcision is a cutting away of the foreskin. It was a ceremony given to Abraham and passed on to all Israel as a sign of the covenant between God and Abraham (Rom. 4:11; Gen. 17:11). Circumcision was to take place when a child was eight days old. Abraham was first told to circumcise himself and all the males of his house in Genesis 17:10-14. So, Abraham's justification (Gen. 15) happened *before* he was circumcised.

The extent to which God granted the blessing of justification is found in verses 9-16.

9 ¶Cometh this blessedness then upon the circumcision only, or upon the uncircumcision also? for we say that faith was reckoned to Abraham for righteousness.
10 How was it then reckoned? when he was in circumcision, or in uncircumcision? Not in circumcision, but in uncircumcision.
11 And he received the sign of circumcision, a seal of the righteousness of the faith which he had yet being uncircumcised: that he might be the father of all them that believe, though they be not circumcised; that righteousness might be imputed unto them also:
12 And the father of circumcision to them who are not of the circumcision only, but who also walk in the steps of that faith of our father Abraham, which he had being yet uncircumcised.
13 For the promise, that he should be the heir of the world, was not to Abraham, or to his seed, through the law, but through the righteousness of faith.
14 For if they which are of the law be heirs, faith is made void, and the promise made of none effect:
15 Because the law worketh wrath: for where no law is, there is no transgression.
16 Therefore it is of faith, that it might be by grace; to the end the promise might be sure to all the seed; not to that only which is of the law, but to that also which is of the faith of Abraham; who is the father of us all (Romans 4:9-16).

Justification is not only for those who are circumcised (the Jews), but it is also for those who are uncircumcised (the Gentiles). This is affirmed by the fact that Abraham was justified before he was circumcised. Circumcision had nothing whatsoever to do with justification. The only requirement for justification is faith in the Lord Jesus Christ. Therefore, Abraham is the spiritual father of all who believe in the Lord Jesus Christ, whether they are circumcised or uncircumcised.

Justification flows from a promise God gave Abraham, "that he should be the heir of the world" (Romans 4:13). Galatians speaks of the promise in these terms, "And the scripture, foreseeing that God would justify the heathen through faith, preached before the gospel unto Abraham, saying, In thee shall all nations be blessed" (Gal. 3:8). According to Galatians 3:16, this promise is fulfilled through Christ: "Now to Abraham and his seed were the promises made. He saith not, And to seeds, as of many; but as of one, And to thy seed, which is Christ." The promise came before circumcision and before the Law. Therefore, it was not fulfilled by the Law, but through the righteousness of faith, that is, justification.

According to Romans 4:13-16, three facts stand out clearly:

> 1) The promise is not through the Law. "For the promise, that he should be the heir of the world, was not to Abraham, or to his seed, through the law, but through the righteousness of faith" (v. 13).

2) The Law makes faith void. "For if they which are of the law be heirs, faith is made void, and the promise made of none effect" (v. 14).
3) The Law works wrath. It shows us we have sinned and are guilty. Sin brings God's wrath. "Because the law worketh wrath: for where no law is, there is no transgression" (v. 15).

In the final analysis, justification is by faith so that it can be by grace. This makes the believer secure in God's promise of salvation, regardless of whether they are a Jew or a Gentile.

Abraham's justification is further explained in Romans 4:17-22.

> 17 ¶(As it is written, I have made thee a father of many nations,) before him whom he believed, even God, who quickeneth the dead, and calleth those things which be not as though they were.
> 18 Who against hope believed in hope, that he might become the father of many nations, according to that which was spoken, So shall thy seed be.
> 19 And being not weak in faith, he considered not his own body now dead, when he was about an hundred years old, neither yet the deadness of Sara's womb:
> 20 He staggered not at the promise of God through unbelief; but was strong in faith, giving glory to God;
> 21 And being fully persuaded that, what he had

> *promised, he was able also to perform.*
> *22 And therefore it was imputed to him for righteousness.*

Abraham was one hundred years old in Genesis fifteen and Sarah was ninety. Yet, when God promised him a son, Abraham was "fully persuaded that, what he had promised, he was able also to perform" (Rom. 4:21). This description of Abraham's faith echoes Paul's declaration in 2 Timothy 1:12, "For the which cause I also suffer these things: nevertheless I am not ashamed: for I know whom I have believed, and am persuaded that he is able to keep that which I have committed unto him against that day." Therefore, he was justified.

The chapter concludes with two final points in Rom. 4:23-25.

> *23 ¶Now it was not written for his sake alone, that it was imputed to him;*
> *24 But for us also, to whom it shall be imputed, if we believe on him that raised up Jesus our Lord from the dead;*
> *25 Who was delivered for our offences, and was raised again for our justification.*

First, there is an assurance that these truths were not just good for Abraham, but for us also. We too will be justified if we believe in the Lord Jesus Christ. Second, the foundation of justification and the object of faith is the gospel of Jesus Christ, "Who was delivered for our offences, and was raised again for our justification." This last statement is a reminder of the essential points of the gospel. We are sinners and Christ died for our sins. Three days later He rose physically from the grave. The resurrection is an absolute essential in any presentation of the gospel. Too often it is left out of gospel tracts. Often the death of Christ is mentioned, but not the resurrection.

Reconciliation – The Result of Justification
Romans 5:1-21

Chapter five presents the benefits of justification. "Therefore being justified by faith, we have peace with God through our Lord Jesus Christ" (Rom. 5:1). Previously, before being justified, we were enemies of God. Now we are no longer enemies, but rather friends of God. "For if, when we were enemies, we were reconciled to God by the death of his Son, much more, being reconciled, we shall be saved by his life" (Rom. 5:10). The Scripture tells us that once we believe the gospel, we become "a new creature: old things are passed away; behold, all things are become new" (2 Cor. 5:17). Because the old life is gone and we have a new life, we can face the future with a new attitude and new blessings. For example, we have new hope in which we can rejoice (v. 2), we shall be saved from wrath (v. 9), and we shall be saved by His life, a fact that looks forward to the resurrection (v. 10).

> 1 Therefore being justified by faith, we have peace with God through our Lord Jesus Christ:
> 2 By whom also we have access by faith into this grace wherein we stand, and rejoice in hope of

> *the glory of God.*
> *3 And not only so, but we glory in tribulations also: knowing that tribulation worketh patience;*
> *4 And patience, experience; and experience, hope:*
> *5 And hope maketh not ashamed; because the love of God is shed abroad in our hearts by the Holy Ghost which is given unto us.* (Rom. 5:1-5)

The *blessings of reconciliation* covered in verses one through five begin with "peace with God." There are two types of peace for the child of God: the peace *of* God (Phil. 4:6-7), which is a trust in God that gives settled peace of mind and heart. The other peace is the peace that follows the end of a war. We have been at war with God, now we are at peace with Him. The latter peace is meant here and is a result of reconciliation with God, although peace of mind is also a result of reconciliation. Second, we have "access" to God. We have unfettered freedom to approach God at any time. The Bible says, "Let us therefore come boldly unto the throne of grace, that we may obtain mercy, and find grace to help in time of need" (Heb. 4:16). We never had that before. Finally, even trouble (tribulation) produces blessings (vv. 3-5) for the person who is a "new creature." So much so, the Bible says we "glory" in tribulation (v. 3). Tribulation, which is often called *temptation,* is used by God to test and purify our faith. The Book of James states, "My brethren, count it all joy when ye fall into divers temptations; knowing this, that the trying of your faith worketh patience. But let patience have her perfect work, that ye may be perfect and entire, wanting nothing" (James

1:2-4). In a similar fashion, Romans 5:3-5 tells us that tribulation brings patience, experience, and hope.

Regarding patience, the Lord Jesus said, "In your patience possess ye your souls (Luke 21:19). Most major issues in life do not require quick emergency type decisions. Patience gives you time to reflect, pray, and search the Scriptures. Then you can make wise decisions. "He that handleth a matter wisely shall find good" (Prov. 16:20). Hasty decisions are often disastrous. "The thoughts of the diligent tend only to plenteousness; but of every one that is hasty only to want" (Prov. 21:5).

Patience results in experience. Laban told Jacob, "I have learned by experience that the LORD hath blessed me for thy sake" (Gen. 30:27). Solomon, in Ecclesiastes 1:16 said, "Yea, my heart had great experience of wisdom and knowledge." As we seek to learn and follow God's will in the journey of life, we will gain much insight into the way God works in different circumstances. That in turn will increase our faith and enable us to go through greater challenges. Much of that experience will open our eyes as to how Scripture applies to the issues of life.

One other thing that experience produces is hope. Our hope is the coming of our Lord Jesus Christ ("Looking for that blessed hope, and the glorious appearing of the great God and our Saviour Jesus Christ"-Titus 2:13), eternal life ("That being justified by his grace, we should be made heirs according to the hope of eternal life"-Titus 3:7), and the Lord Jesus, Himself (I Tim. 1:1). According to Romans 5:2 and other verses (e.g. Eph. 1) this is all to the glory of God and our hope is in that glory. Our hope is not wishful thinking. It is sure and certain. We can't see it now, but we have an inner certainty from the Spirit of God (Rom. 8:24-25). The results of hope are confidence and love and joy (Rom. 5:2).

Foundation of reconciliation
Romans 5:6-11

6 ¶For when we were yet without strength, in due time Christ died for the ungodly.
7 For scarcely for a righteous man will one die: yet peradventure for a good man some would even dare to die.
8 But God commendeth his love toward us, in that, while we were yet sinners, Christ died for us.
9 Much more then, being now justified by his blood, we shall be saved from wrath through him.
10 For if, when we were enemies, we were reconciled to God by the death of his Son, much more, being reconciled, we shall be saved by his life.
11 And not only so, but we also joy in God through our Lord Jesus Christ, by whom we have now received the atonement.

Before we were reconciled, we were without strength (v. 6), ungodly (v. 6), sinners (v. 8), and enemies (v. 10). Now we are justified and reconciled by His death (v. 6), by His love (v. 8), by His blood (v. 9), and, being reconciled, we will be "saved by his life" (v. 10). Now, we have joy as a result of having received the "atonement" (v. 11). The Greek word for *atonement* here is the same word that is translated as *reconciliation* elsewhere. So, as used here "atonement" is a synonym for reconciliation. According to Thayer and Eastman's Bible Dictionary it means "restoration to favor," the state of being at one with another. We were God's enemies, separated from Hum. Now, we have been restored to God's favor and united with Him. We are now His friends and part of His family.

Why Reconciliation is Needed – the Two Adams
Romans 5:12-21

12 Wherefore, as by one man sin entered into the world, and death by sin; and so death passed upon all men, for that all have sinned:
13 (For until the law sin was in the world: but sin is not imputed when there is no law.
14 Nevertheless death reigned from Adam to Moses, even over them that had not sinned after the similitude of Adam's transgression, who is the figure of him that was to come.
15 But not as the offence, so also is the free gift. For if through the offence of one many be dead, much more the grace of God, and the gift by grace, which is by one man, Jesus Christ, hath abounded unto many.
16 And not as it was by one that sinned, so is the gift: for the judgment was by one to condemnation, but the free gift is of many offences unto justification.
17 For if by one man's offence death reigned by one; much more they which receive abundance of grace and of the gift of righteousness shall reign in life by one, Jesus Christ.)
18 Therefore as by the offence of one judgment came upon all men to condemnation; even so by the righteousness of one the free gift came upon all men unto justification of life.
19 For as by one man's disobedience many were made sinners, so by the obedience of one shall many be made

righteous.
20 Moreover the law entered, that the offence might abound. But where sin abounded, grace did much more abound:
21 That as sin hath reigned unto death, even so might grace reign through righteousness unto eternal life by Jesus Christ our Lord.

In this section, God lays out the basic historical and theological reasons why mankind is in such a terrible spiritual condition. These reasons are why we need reconciliation with God. The reasons lie in a contrast between Adam and Christ, who is called the "last Adam" (1 Cor. 15:45). One man brought sin and all its consequences into the world. The second man brought eternal life into the world in response to the presence of sin. What Adam caused to go wrong, Jesus Christ set right. God knew that Adam would fail and He allowed it, but He set it all right through Christ. John Gill (1697-1771), a well-known English Baptist pastor, [15] said:

> **Romans 5:12-Wherefore as by one man sin entered into the world....** The design of these words, and of the following, is to show how men came to be in the condition before described, as "ungodly", Rom. 5:6, "sinners", Rom. 5:8, and "enemies", Rom. 5:10; and to express the love of Christ in the redemption of them; and the largeness of God's grace to all sorts of men: the connection of them is with Rom. 5:11, by which it appears that the saints have not only an

expiation of sin by the blood of Christ, but a perfect righteousness, by which they are justified in the sight of God; and the manner how they came at it, or this becomes theirs, together with the necessity of their having such an one, are here declared. [16]

The first general principle is that when sin entered the world, death also entered the world. Another principle states that if there is no Law, there is no transgression (v. 13; 4:15). Sin was in the world between Adam and Moses, who gave the law, but given this principle sin is not counted to people when there is no law (v. 13). Regardless, the Bible says in verse 14, death still prevailed, even on those who had not sinned the same way Adam did. How was that? Adam violated a direct explicit commandment given to Him from the lips of God. In other words, Adam violated the law of God. There were no other explicit commands given until God told Noah to build an ark (Genesis 6), although everyman had a sense of right and wrong in their conscience and they had the witness of the creation and the stories of creation and Adam's fall. So, the consequences brought to mankind by the sin of Adam, the father of the human race, were real and present regardless of whether people sinned against an explicit command of God or not.

The following table shows the contrast between Adam and the free gift of God in Jesus Christ. The "gift" is mentioned seven times in this passage. It is defined as "the gift of righteousness," (v. 17) which is given by the grace of God (v. 15).

Verse	In Adam – the Offense	In Christ – the Free Gift
15	One man leads many to death	One man leads many to the gift and to life
16	One offense to condemnation	Many offenses to justification
17	By one offense death reigned	By one man many reign in life
18	One offense= condemnation on ALL	One man offers justification to ALL
19	One man's disobedience=many sinners	One man's obedience=many made righteous
20	Law makes offenses abundantly clear	The greater the sin-the more grace God gives
21	Sin reigned to death	Grace reigns through righteousness to eternal life

Table 2

When all one has is sin, death, and the Law and all you have to look forward to is condemnation, the situation is clearly desperate. When you find that God offers life, justification, and grace with the promise of eternal life, the only rational decision is to be reconciled to God through faith in Jesus Christ. The only way to escape our condition and condemnation for our sinful actions is to be reconciled to God and receive the gift of justification.

Chapter Three

The Sanctification of Believers
Romans 6:1-8:16

Once a person puts faith in the Lord Jesus and receives justification and is reconciled to God, the next step is sanctification. The word sanctify means "to separate from profane things and dedicate to God ... consecrate things to God ... dedicate people to God ... to purify ... to purify by expiation: free from the guilt of sin ... to purify internally by renewing of the soul." [17] W. E. Vine says:

> Sanctification is also used in NT of the separation of the believer from evil things and ways. This sanctification is God's will for the believer, 1Thess. 4:3, and His purpose in calling him by the gospel, 1Thess. 4:7; it must be learned from God, 1Thess. 4:4, as He teaches it by His Word, John 17:17, John 17:19, cf. Ps. 17:4; Ps. 119:9,

and it must be pursued by the believer, earnestly and undeviatingly, 1Tim. 2:15; Heb. 12:14. [18]

In one sense of the word, sanctification happens immediately when one trusts Christ. For example, 1 Cor. 1:2 addresses the Christians in Corinth as those who "are sanctified in Christ Jesus, called to be saints." The term "sanctified" in that verse is in the Greek perfect tense. The perfect tense speaks of an action that took place in the past and is still true or still has current effects. In this case, they were sanctified when they trusted Christ and they are still sanctified. This is sometimes referred to as the *position* we occupy in Christ. It is freely conferred on us by God's grace the same as justification is a free gift of God's grace. Because of this position we occupy, we are called *saints*. Sanctification is the state of being separated to God, that is, to be holy to God. A saint is a separated one, a holy one. All believers are saints.

Sanctification also has a present tense application. When we trust Christ, we are justified, reconciled, and set apart to God (sanctified). But, our lives and characters are not yet purified and perfected. We still have sinful habits and practices and weaknesses of character that God wants to change. Therefore, we need a *process* of sanctification. 1 Thessalonians 4:3-4 says that sanctification is a process of separating your practical everyday life from sin. In that case, the example given is staying away from fornication. Some day, when the Lord gives us our resurrected body, we will be set apart, from sin altogether. It will no longer have any presence in us.

The term "salvation" is used in a similar manner and means "deliverance from sin." [19] Eternal salvation is granted immediately upon our faith in Christ (Acts 2:47; 11:14; 16:30-31; Rom. 1:16; 1 Cor. 1:18; 2 Cor. 2:15). We must also be saved from the power of sin in our daily lives (Phil. 2:12). Finally, we will be saved from the very presence of sin (Rom. 13:11; 1 Thess. 5:8-90; Heb. 1:14). Salvation is very similar in meaning to sanctification. You can see this graphically in Table 3.

Tenses of Salvation

Three Tenses	Salvation/Sanctification	Effect
Past salvation/sanctification	Justification/ separated to God as His possession/ made saints	Saved from the penalty of sin
Present salvation/sanctification	Sanctification-growth in practical obedience and holiness	Saved from the power of sin
Future salvation/sanctification	Glorification- transformed to be like Christ-given a sinless body	Saved from the presence of sin

Table 3

The section of Romans we are about to examine is all about daily practical sanctification. Chapter six lays the foundation for sanctification. There are some additional things, not mentioned yet, that God does for us when we trust Christ. These things make it possible for us to overcome our natural fleshly tendencies and live a life that pleases God. Chapter seven explains the conflict between the Law and the flesh. It is a conflict that makes the Law ineffective in producing righteousness and it is a conflict that creates difficulties in Christian living. Chapter 8 shows that we can overcome this conflict through the Spirit of God. We can overcome the conflict only by dependence on the power of the Spirit of God which resides in us.

In the Likeness of His Death and Resurrection
Romans 6:1-23

The theme of Romans 6:1-8:16 is stated in verses one and two, "What shall we say then? Shall we continue in sin, that grace may abound? God forbid. How shall we, that are dead to sin, live any longer therein?" Before we were saved by God's grace through faith (Eph. 2:8-9), we were spiritually dead in trespasses and sins (Eph. 2:2). At that time, we were dominated by the devil, the world, and the flesh, our sinful nature (Eph. 2:2-3). It was necessary that God do something to free us from the domination of these influences and make it possible for us to live a consistently obedient Christian life. When we trusted Christ, we were born again. It was our spirits which were born (John 3:3, 6). This was part of God's solution and gives us the opportunity to "walk in newness of life" (v. 4).

Romans 6 supplies us with four basic steps or principles and a warning in the process of sanctification. The steps are as follows:

1) We need to *KNOW* some things (Rom. 6:2-10).
2) We need to *RECKON* something to be true (Rom. 6:11).
3) We must *NOT YIELD* to unrighteousness (Rom. 6:12-13a).
4) We must *YIELD* to God (Rom. 6:13b-14).
5) Heed this *WARNING* (Rom. 6:15-23).

We need to *KNOW* some things.
(Rom. 6:2-10)

1 What shall we say then? Shall we continue in sin, that grace may abound? God forbid. How shall we, that are dead to sin, live any longer therein?
2 God forbid. How shall we, that are dead to sin, live any longer therein?
3 Know ye not, that so many of us as were baptized into Jesus Christ were baptized into his death?
4 Therefore we are buried with him by baptism into death: that like as Christ was raised up from the dead by the glory of the Father, even so we also should walk in newness of life.
5 For if we have been planted together in the likeness of his death, we shall be also in the likeness of his resurrection:
6 Knowing this, that our old man is crucified with him, that the body of sin might be destroyed, that henceforth we should not serve sin.
7 For he that is dead is freed from sin.
8 Now if we be dead with Christ, we believe that we shall also live with him:

9 Knowing that Christ being raised from the dead dieth no more; death hath no more dominion over him.
10 For in that he died, he died unto sin once: but in that he liveth, he liveth unto God.

"**Know** ye not, that so many of us as were baptized into Jesus Christ were baptized into his death?" (Rom. 6:3) This verse along with verse four, "we are buried with him by baptism into death," begins to answer the question in verse two, "How shall we, that are dead to sin, live any longer therein?" It brings to mind the verse in Colossians 3:3, "For ye are dead, and your life is hid with Christ in God" and Galatians 2:20, "I am crucified with Christ: nevertheless I live; yet not I, but Christ liveth in me: and the life which I now live in the flesh I live by the faith of the Son of God, who loved me, and gave himself for me." This is, of course, exactly what Paul is talking about in Romans 6:2-10, because verse six says, "**Knowing** this, that our old man is crucified with him ..."

It should be noted right away that the baptism spoken of in verses three and four cannot possibly be water baptism. This baptism puts us "into Jesus Christ" and "into his death." There is no water anywhere in the world that can do that. Remember that John the Baptist said of Jesus, "I indeed baptize you with water unto repentance: but he that cometh after me is mightier than I, whose shoes I am not worthy to bear: he shall baptize you with the Holy Ghost" (Mt. 3:11). The Baptism of Romans 6:3-4 is the Baptism of the Holy Ghost. The baptism of the Spirit puts us into the body of Christ, the church, when we get saved (1 Cor. 12:13; Eph. 1:22-23), as well as uniting us with the death of Christ on the cross: "For by one Spirit are we all baptized into one body, whether we be Jews or Gentiles, whether we be bond or free; and have been all made to drink into one Spirit" (1 Cor. 12:13). It is evident, then, that the baptism of the Spirit takes place when we first trust Christ. It is not some sort of "second blessing." It is not equivalent to the "filling of the Spirit," which takes place repeatedly at various times throughout the Christian life (Eph. 5:16). It is silent, unseen, and unfelt. But, it makes a profound difference in the soul.

In the view of God, when Christ was crucified on the cross, we were there too. Romans six tells us that "our old man is crucified with him" (v. 6) and the reason for this is so that "the body of sin might be destroyed." The "body of sin" is the same thing that Paul calls "the flesh" elsewhere. It is the part of us where the fallen nature abides. Romans 7:18 says, "For I know that in me (that is, in my flesh,) dwelleth no good thing." The body of sin is not destroyed in the sense of killed or dissolved or ruined. It is destroyed in the sense that it is made ineffective or of no effect. [20] The flesh enslaved us and ruled us as unsaved individuals. We "all had our conversation in times past in the lusts of our flesh, fulfilling the desires of the flesh and of the mind" (cf. Eph. 2:1-3). Now slavery to the flesh has been ended for us who are saved. We are dead in Christ and we have been crucified with Christ so that from the day we got saved onward "we should not serve sin" (v. 6). The fact is that "he that is dead is freed from sin" (v. 7). No dead body needs to worry about sin. It is dead and cannot sin any longer. Even so, we are dead in Christ and the domination of sin in our old lives is over. We are no longer *controlled* by sin.

Our death to sin is not the only thing we need to know. *We also need to know that we are alive to God.* We are told "that like as Christ was raised up from the dead by the glory of the Father, even so we also should walk in newness of life" (v. 4) and "if we have been planted together in the likeness of his death, we shall be also in the likeness of his resurrection" (v. 5) and "Now if we be dead with Christ, we believe that we shall also live with him" (v. 8) and "reckon ye also yourselves to be dead indeed unto sin, but alive unto God through Jesus Christ our Lord" (v. 11). We are born again by His Spirit (John 3:6). We are new creatures in Christ (2 Cor. 5:17). We have the very life and power of God at work in us (Eph. 3:20). We have Christ Himself living within us (Col. 1:27). His presence and the life now living in us, makes our death to sin and our new life a reality. The flesh has been a tyrannical slave master over us. Now the slave is free – free from slavery to sin and free to live a new life in the power of God. Ultimately, as these verses say, this will culminate in a new eternal physical life at the resurrection (Rom. 6:4-5). We must know this.

We need to *RECKON* these things to be true (Rom. 6:11)

Likewise reckon ye also yourselves to be dead indeed unto sin, but alive unto God through Jesus Christ our Lord (Rom. 6:11).

The word "reckon" means to consider. We must consider ourselves to be dead to sin and alive to God. To recon it, we must *believe* that it is true. Most of us would find it hard to believe that we are dead to sin and free from sin. Nevertheless, that is exactly what the Bible says is true. When we look at ourselves, we see a tendency to think impure or unkind thoughts, to have sinful wishes or desires, to go where we shouldn't, or to do what we shouldn't. It is painfully obvious to us that the flesh is still there and is still operating full steam. How can we be dead to sin and alive to God? Regardless of these experiences, the Bible says we are indeed dead to sin and alive to God. *This is true whether we believe it or not.* We must embrace this truth. It takes a step of faith, but we must accept what the Bible says about us to be true. This is a necessary step toward living an obedient Christian life. It is also not a onetime thing, as if we say it to ourselves once and that is enough. No, we must habitually, daily reckon ourselves to be dead to sin and alive to God. We count on this and rely on it to help us live obedient lives. [21]

We must not *YIELD* to sin
We must, rather, *YIELD* to God
(Rom. 6:12-14)

12 Let not sin therefore reign in your mortal body, that ye should obey it in the lusts thereof.
13 Neither yield ye your members as instruments of unrighteousness unto sin: but yield yourselves unto God, as those that are alive from the dead, and your members as instruments of righteousness unto God.
14 For sin shall not have dominion over you: for ye are not under the law, but under grace. (Rom. 6:12-14).

Even though we have been freed from slavery to the sin nature, the flesh is still there. It still wants to dominate us. It's still possible to yield to the lust of the flesh and commit sins. Obedience is not automatic simply because we are dead to sin, alive to God, and therefore free to live holy lives. Temptation will occur and failure is possible. We must choose to exercise our freedom. We do not have to yield to temptation and sin. When Abraham Lincoln issued the Emancipation Proclamation and made it good by winning the Civil War, the slaves in the south were free. However, they had to assert their freedom. They could have chosen to continue obeying an intimidating "master" or they could embrace their freedom and turn away from him who was no longer their master.

Temptation to sin has its source in our own desires. "But every man is tempted, when he is drawn away of his own lust, and enticed. Then when lust hath conceived, it bringeth forth sin: and sin, when it is finished, bringeth forth death. Do not err, my beloved brethren" (James 1:14-16). This is why the Lord exhorted us to deny ourselves (Lk. 9:23). The counterbalance to the lust of the flesh is love for God. It is this heart of love for God that moves us to deny ourselves. We love the Lord so much and want to please Him so much more than we want to please ourselves. "And thou shalt love the Lord thy God with all thy heart, and with all thy soul, and with all thy mind, and with all thy strength: this is the first commandment" (Mk. 12:30). This is one of the reasons we need to spend time in prayer and reading the Word of God. It is necessary that we cultivate a heart of worship toward the Lord.

We can view these things as *steps* to take. The first step is to know that we are dead to the sin nature and alive to God. The second step is to believe it and to reckon it to be true. The third step is to refuse to yield to sin. The Scripture says to not yield "your members as instruments of unrighteousness unto sin." It is a command to keep ourselves from participating in sinful activities of any kind. It requires keeping control of the impulses of the body. It is also a decision. We must choose to not give in to sin. In his book *The Pursuit of Holiness,* pages 54 and 55, Jerry Bridges said:

> The first thing we should notice in this passage is that the pursuit of holiness – this not allowing sin to reign in our mortal bodies – is something *we* have to do. Paul's statement is one of exhortation. He addressed himself to our wills. He said, "Do not let sin reign." Implying that this is something for which we ourselves are responsible. The experience of holiness is not a gift we receive like justification, but something we are clearly exhorted to work at. [22]

Please note that even though we are exhorted to work at yielding and obedience, the Christian life is a life of *faith.* "The just shall live by faith" (Rom. 1:17). We do not work at yielding with any faith in *ourselves*. Our faith is in the power of God exercised in our lives by the Holy Spirit. Jesus said, "Without me you can do nothing" (John 15:5). On the other hand, "I can do all things through Christ which strengtheneth me" (Phil. 4:13) and, "Not that we are sufficient of ourselves to think anything as of ourselves; but our sufficiency is of God" (2 Cor. 3:5). Since, "faith cometh by hearing, and hearing by the word of God" (Rom. 10:17), we must believe everything God has said. We have to believe His promises, but we need to believe His commands, also. If we trust His commands, we will be far more eager to follow them and obey.

The next step is to positively yield to God (v. 13). It is not enough to choose to resist sin. We must also *choose* to obey God. We resist sin because we are dead to sin and, therefore, free from sin. However, we yield to God because we are "alive from the dead." The new life that is in us moves us to love God. Jesus said, "He that hath my commandments, and keepeth them, he it is that loveth me" (John 14:21). There are at least three reasons why we must yield to God.

The first reason we should not yield to sin, but rather yield to God is that we are free from the law (Rom. 6:14, 15). It is by the Law that sin has dominion over us. The Law makes us know what sin is (Rom. 7:7). It makes us guilty before God, a guilt that is designed to cause us to come to Christ (Gal. 3:24). Yet, the imposition of the Law also seems to incite sinful impulses and increase the difficulty of holy living (Rom. 7:8). "But sin, taking occasion by the commandment, wrought in me all manner of concupiscence. For without the law sin was dead" (Rom. 7:8). Nevertheless, the Law is the expression of God's will and, therefore, it is holy, just, good, and spiritual (Rom. 7:12-14). When Christ died on the cross, He removed the Law from being an obstacle to us. He "abolished in his flesh the enmity, even the law of commandments contained in ordinances" (Eph.

2:15). Colossians 2:13-14 puts it this way, "And you, being dead in your sins and the uncircumcision of your flesh, hath he quickened together with him, having forgiven you all trespasses; Blotting out the handwriting of ordinances that was against us, which was contrary to us, and took it out of the way, nailing it to his cross."

A Final Warning
(Rom. 6:15-23)

15 What then? shall we sin, because we are not under the law, but under grace? God forbid .
16 Know ye not, that to whom ye yield yourselves servants to obey, his servants ye are to whom ye obey; whether of sin unto death, or of obedience unto righteousness?
(Rom. 6:15-16)

    Though we are free from the Law, we are absolutely not free to sin (v. 15). "But now we are delivered from the law, that being dead wherein we were held; that we should serve in newness of spirit, and not in the oldness of the letter" (Rom. 7:6). Freedom from the Law makes us free to serve God out of love for Him, not just out of duty to the Law. We have a living heart-to-heart relationship with the Lord. We respond to Him out of our hearts and spirits. Our obedience is not a matter of following a dead cold set of ordinances, but of seeking to please one we love. So, we should never think that freedom from the Law is freedom to sin. Freedom from the law gives us freedom from guilt, freedom from condemnation, but never freedom to sin.

The second reason we must yield to God rather than to sin is that we will be once more in bondage if we yield to sin (v. 16). The Scripture says we become a servant to whom we yield. A Christian can even become addicted to certain sins because he has made a habit of yielding to temptation. This is how Christians can be "overtaken in a fault" (Gal. 6:1). This type of bondage can be harder to overcome than it was to break old sinful habits right after we were saved.

This is all a process of growth that is illustrated in Colossians 3:1-17 as a process of changing clothes.

> *If ye then be risen with Christ, seek those things which are above, where Christ sitteth on the right hand of God. Set your affection on things above, not on things on the earth. For ye are dead, and your life is hid with Christ in God. When Christ, who is our life, shall appear, then shall ye also appear with him in glory.* **Mortify therefore** *your members which are upon the earth; fornication, uncleanness, inordinate affection, evil concupiscence, and covetousness, which is idolatry: For which things' sake the wrath of God cometh on the children of disobedience: In the which ye also walked some time, when ye lived in them. But now ye also* **put off** *all these; anger, wrath, malice, blasphemy, filthy communication out of your mouth. Lie not one to another, seeing that ye have put off the old man with his deeds; And have put on the new man, which is renewed in knowledge after the*

image of him that created him: Where there is neither Greek nor Jew, circumcision nor uncircumcision, Barbarian, Scythian, bond nor free: but Christ is all, and in all. **Put on therefore**, *as the elect of God, holy and beloved, bowels of mercies, kindness, humbleness of mind, meekness, longsuffering; Forbearing one another, and forgiving one another, if any man have a quarrel against any: even as Christ forgave you, so also do ye. And above all these things put on charity, which is the bond of perfectness. And let the peace of God rule in your hearts, to the which also ye are called in one body; and be ye thankful. Let the word of Christ dwell in you richly in all wisdom; teaching and admonishing one another in psalms and hymns and spiritual songs, singing with grace in your hearts to the Lord. And whatsoever ye do in word or deed, do all in the name of the Lord Jesus, giving thanks to God and the Father by him.*

When we obey God we also become servants to righteousness:

17 But God be thanked, that ye were the servants of sin, but ye have obeyed from the heart that form of doctrine which was delivered you.
18 Being then made free from sin, ye became the servants of righteousness.

> *19 I speak after the manner of men because of the infirmity of your flesh: for as ye have yielded your members servants to uncleanness and to iniquity unto iniquity; even so now yield your members servants to righteousness unto holiness.*
> (Rom. 6:17-19)

When God saves us, He makes us *free* from sin (v. 18). When we obey God from the heart (v. 17), we become the servants of righteousness (v. 18). Nevertheless, the warning still stands. If we yield to sin, we become the servants of sin. It all depends largely on the choices we make. We have all been spiritually and sinfully dirty in various ways. Now, go a different direction. Don't follow the old habits of life that were dictated by the flesh. Now, follow God in obedient and righteous living that leads to true holiness of life.

A third reason not to yield to sin, but yield to God is because the fruit of yielding to sin is harmful and shameful (v. 20- 21).

> *20 For when ye were the servants of sin, ye were free from righteousness.*
> *21 What fruit had ye then in those things whereof ye are now ashamed? for the end of those things is death.*
> *22 But now being made free from sin, and become servants to God, ye have your fruit unto holiness, and the end everlasting life.*
> *23 For the wages of sin is death; but the gift of*

God is eternal life through Jesus Christ our Lord.

Chapter six ends on a positive note. There is rejoicing that we became the servants of God and righteousness when we trusted Christ. It was a great contrast to the life we led before. So, Paul asks, what was the fruit from that life? The final end of that life was death- both physical death and death in Hell. However, the fruit of a life serving God is holiness and the end is everlasting life (v. 22).

The Battle for Obedience Continues to Rage
Romans 7:1-25

1 Know ye not, brethren, (for I speak to them that know the law,) how that the law hath dominion over a man as long as he liveth?
2 For the woman which hath an husband is bound by the law to her husband so long as he liveth; but if the husband be dead, she is loosed from the law of her husband.
3 So then if, while her husband liveth, she be married to another man, she shall be called an adulteress: but if her husband be dead, she is free from that law; so that she is no adulteress, though she be married to another man.
4 Wherefore, my brethren, ye also are become dead to the law by the body of Christ; that ye should be married to another, even to him who is raised from the dead, that we should bring forth fruit unto God.
5 For when we were in the flesh, the motions of sins, which were by the law, did work in our members to bring forth fruit

unto death.
6 But now we are delivered from the law, that being dead wherein we were held; that we should serve in newness of spirit, and not in the oldness of the letter. (Rom. 7:1-6)

Romans 7 starts out by once again stating that we are free from the law. This is illustrated from marriage. The Law binds a woman to her spouse until death. Once the spouse dies then she is free from the law of marriage and may marry another. Similarly, we are dead to the Law and, therefore, we can be married or united to Christ without the law. The result of this is that we can serve God from our spirits, not from a mere obligation to law. This causes us to produce spiritual fruit to the glory of God.

The Law is Good (Rom. 7:7-13)

7 What shall we say then? Is the law sin? God forbid. Nay, I had not known sin, but by the law: for I had not known lust, except the law had said, Thou shalt not covet.
8 But sin, taking occasion by the commandment, wrought in me all manner of concupiscence. For without the law sin was dead.
9 For I was alive without the law once: but when the commandment came, sin revived, and I died.
10 And the commandment, which was ordained to life, I found to be unto death.
11 For sin, taking occasion by the commandment, deceived me, and by it slew me.
12 Wherefore the law is holy, and the commandment holy, and just, and good.

13 Was then that which is good made death unto me? God forbid. But sin, that it might appear sin, working death in me by that which is good; that sin by the commandment might become exceeding sinful. (Rom. 7:7-13)

It is important that we understand the nature and the purpose of the Law. It would be easy to belittle it and think that it has no purpose in a Christian's life. Such is not the case. The Law is holy, righteous, and good (v. 12). It is the Law of God. It was given by God to Moses (e.g. Ex. 20). The Law was given for a purpose and has a profound effect on human beings.

The purpose of the Law is to change the perspective of an individual toward his own personal sin. It was given so that "sin by the commandment might become exceeding sinful" (v. 13). It's not that sin isn't sinful. Before we were saved and before we knew the Law, we were not aware of the destructive force that was within us. When the Law made us to understand the sin that is in us and the sin that we have committed, it suddenly appears as exceeding sinful *to us*. The saying becomes true in us: "*I had not known sin, but by the law*" (Rom. 7:7).

Further, the passage says that sin is dead without the law. We were, according to verse 9, alive once, "*without the law*" (v. 8), but "when the commandment came, sin revived, and I died" (v. 9). It is possible that a child is alive spiritually until the Law of God is revealed to his conscience and he dies spiritually. This may be true. However, I think it more likely that here we are looking at an individual perception (in this case, Paul's). Before being aware of how the Law speaks to his own sin, he *feels* alive and secure and sometimes almost at peace with his sin. When the Holy Spirit convicts him of sin, righteousness, and judgment (John 16:7-11), his whole outlook changes. He knows himself to be sinful and dirty. When a person accepts and embraces this conviction, it is repentance. Sin is transgression of the law (1 John 3:4). When the law comes to a person, sin is suddenly put in the light and shows up as exceeding sinful.

This is a good thing. The purpose of the law is put another way in Galatians 3:24, "Wherefore the law was our schoolmaster to bring us unto Christ, that we might be justified by faith." The purpose of the law is to show us how sinful we are and to point us to the gospel of the Lord Jesus Christ as the only cure for our sinful condition.

The Raging Conflict (Rom. 7:14-23)

14 For we know that the law is spiritual: but I am carnal, sold under sin.
15 For that which I do I allow not: for what I would, that do I not; but what I hate, that do I.
16 If then I do that which I would not, I consent unto the law that it is good.
17 Now then it is no more I that do it, but sin that dwelleth in me.
18 For I know that in me (that is, in my flesh,) dwelleth no good thing: for to will is present with me; but how to perform that which is good I find not.
19 For the good that I would I do not: but the evil which I would not, that I do.
20 Now if I do that I would not, it is no more I that do it, but sin that dwelleth in me.

21 I find then a law, that, when I would do good, evil is present with me.
22 For I delight in the law of God after the inward man:
23 But I see another law in my members, warring against the law of my mind, and bringing me into captivity to the law of sin which is in my members.

The result of sin is death (v. 9-13; 6:23). We are dead spiritually in trespasses and sins (Eph. 2:1-3). Physical death was brought into the world by sin (Rom. 5). Someday sin will lead to eternal death in the lake of fire (Rev. 20:11-15). However, "the law of the Spirit of life in Christ Jesus hath made me free from the law of sin and death" (Rom. 8:2).

Even though we are now dead to sin and alive to God, we believe it, and we reckon it to be true, we still find ourselves pulled toward sin. Although, we are free from the Law and we should bring forth fruit to God (Rom. 7:1-13), we find ourselves experiencing lust and disobedience. There seems to still be something wrong inside. There seems to be a conflict going on within us. One part wants to serve and obey God, but another part wants do wrong – to do what it wants rather than what God wants. Temptation, itself, comes from a desire to do wrong. "But every man is tempted, when he is drawn away of his own lust, and enticed" (James 1:14).

Some say that the conflict described in Romans 7:14-23 is not referring the experience of a Christian. I disagree. This conflict is certainly real in our personal experience. It is also described in Galatians 5:17: "For the flesh lusteth against the Spirit, and the Spirit against the flesh: and these are contrary the one to the other: so that ye cannot do the things that ye would." You are caught in the middle of a war. The flesh (the sinful nature) wants one thing and your spirit, which is born again and where the Holy Spirit resides and influences you, wants something different. They both exert a strong influence on you. You "cannot do the things that ye would." You will yield to one or the other. You are dead to sin and alive to God. You are no longer a slave to the flesh. However, the flesh is not powerless. It is still present and active. You do not have to do what sin wants you to do, but sin still wants to control you. It is you who makes the decision. Too often, we choose to let sin control us. Romans 7:14-23 explains this conflict.

Paul says he does not allow sin, he hates sin, he wants to do good things, he delights in the Law of God, and he wills to do right. Yet, he also acknowledges that there is a part of him where nothing good dwells and it is that part that exerts a great effort to rule him and his life. So, the result is that he sometimes does the evil he does not want to do, he does that which he does not allow, and he does that which he hates. We often find this struggle to be all too real. We don't *have* to give in to temptation, but we often choose to obey our sinful desire (James 1:14).

You can add to this the attacks by Satan and the influence of the world (Eph. 2:2-3). The Bible says, "Be sober, be vigilant; because your adversary the devil, as a roaring lion, walketh about, seeking whom he may devour" (1 Pet. 5:8). Paul said the devil has various "devices" he uses to lay traps for us (2 Cor. 2:11). The devil also tries to deceive us. Among other things, he will deceive us about our own sinful nature, he will seek to minimize the destructiveness of sinful conduct, and he will lie to us about other people to cause divisions and bitterness. The only answer for this is to know the Word of God. Satan is not the only thing that we must be "vigilant" about. We may have obtained our freedom from sin, but we live in a world full of slaves to sin. Their attitudes and actions are a powerful influence and can affect us in ways of which we are not even aware. Again, the Word of God has the answer.

Paul came to realize that he did not know "how to perform that which is good" (v. 18). He finally cried out, *"O wretched man that I am! Who shall deliver me from the body of this death* (v. 24)?" God wishes us to come to this very point. It is a point of brokenness, a point when we realize with Paul that the answer to this question lies in Jesus Christ, not in us: *"I thank God through Jesus Christ our Lord"* (v. 25). We have no sufficiency for this in ourselves. All our sufficiency comes from Christ (2 Cor. 3:5): "Not that we are sufficient of ourselves to think anything as of ourselves; but our sufficiency is of God." And the Bible further says, "I can do all things *through Christ* which strengtheneth me" (Phil. 4:13). This leads us into Romans 8, which explains how Christ works in us.

Walking "not after the flesh, but after the Spirit"
Romans 8:1-16

Romans 8:1 There is therefore now no condemnation to them which are in Christ Jesus, who walk not after the flesh, but after the Spirit.
2 For the law of the Spirit of life in Christ Jesus hath made me free from the law of sin and death.
3 For what the law could not do, in that it was weak through

the flesh, God sending his own Son in the likeness of sinful flesh, and for sin, condemned sin in the flesh:

4 That the righteousness of the law might be fulfilled in us, who walk not after the flesh, but after the Spirit.

5 For they that are after the flesh do mind the things of the flesh; but they that are after the Spirit the things of the Spirit.

6 For to be carnally minded is death; but to be spiritually minded is life and peace.

7 Because the carnal mind is enmity against God: for it is not subject to the law of God, neither indeed can be.

8 So then they that are in the flesh cannot please God.

9 But ye are not in the flesh, but in the Spirit, if so be that the Spirit of God dwell in you. Now if any man have not the Spirit of Christ, he is none of his.

10 ¶And if Christ be in you, the body is dead because of sin; but the Spirit is life because of righteousness.

11 But if the Spirit of him that raised up Jesus from the dead dwell in you, he that raised up Christ from the dead shall also quicken your mortal bodies by his Spirit that dwelleth in you.

12 Therefore, brethren, we are debtors, not to the flesh, to live after the flesh.

13 For if ye live after the flesh, ye shall die: but if ye through the Spirit do mortify the deeds of the body, ye shall live.

14 For as many as are led by the Spirit of God, they are the sons of God.

15 For ye have not received the spirit of bondage again to fear; but ye have received the Spirit of adoption, whereby we cry, Abba, Father.

16 The Spirit itself beareth witness with our spirit, that we are the children of God:

Romans 8 starts out with no condemnation to those in Christ who walk not after the flesh, but after the Spirit. Is there condemnation then for a Christian, who walks according to the flesh? Verse two says, "For the law of the Spirit of life in Christ Jesus hath made me free from the law of sin and death." The Spirit brings life, but sin brings death as Romans 6:23 says. What is the law of sin and death? Romans 8:13 gives us the answer: "For if ye live after the flesh, ye shall die." The matter of eternal salvation is a settled issue for a believer. There is no eternal condemnation. However, there is the possibility of temporal condemnation to a Christian who fails to walk in obedience to God. Paul cites an example of this when some of the Corinthian believers were abusing the Lord's Supper: "For he that eateth and drinketh unworthily, eateth and drinketh damnation to himself, not discerning the Lord's body. For this cause many are weak and sickly among you, and many *sleep*" (1 Cor. 11:29-30). "Sleep" refers to death. The weak, sickly, and sleep are part of the Lord's chastening (Heb. 12:5-13).

What is the law of the Spirit of life (v. 2)? Once again this is defined in Roman 8:13: "if ye through the Spirit do mortify the deeds of the body, ye shall live." This brings us to our major concern. Given the conflict described in Romans seven, how do we "mortify the deeds of the body?" Galatians 5:16 says, "Walk in the Spirit, and ye shall not fulfill the lust of the flesh." The word "mortify" (Rom. 8:13) means "to subdue or bring into subjection." [23] Romans chapter eight has some principles that help us do that.

The first principle is that Christ fulfills the law in us (v. 3-4). Righteousness cannot be fulfilled through the Law.

The Law demands righteousness, but it offers no power with which to fulfill its requirements. The Law is weak because the flesh is weak and cannot perfectly obey it. In fact, as we saw in Romans seven, the flesh is opposed to the Law in favor of fulfilling its own lusts. There is only one way the righteousness of the Law can be fulfilled by us. That is because Christ dwells in us. One of the great mysteries of the faith is how that Christ lives in us. The Lord Jesus Christ comes with all his wisdom and strength. "But of him are ye in Christ Jesus, who of God is made unto us wisdom, and righteousness, and sanctification, and redemption: That, according as it is written, He that glorieth, let him glory in the Lord" (1 Cor. 1:30-31).

The fact that Christ dwells in us also means that we have the Spirit of God dwelling in us. "So then they that are in the flesh cannot please God. But ye are not in the flesh, but in the Spirit, if so be that the Spirit of God dwell in you. Now if any man have not the Spirit of Christ, he is none of his" (Rom. 8:8-9). The unsaved cannot live obedient and holy lives, but a Christian can because he has the Spirit of God. The presence of the Holy Spirit in us makes God's enormous power available to us. Paul prayed in Colossians 1:11, "Strengthened with all might, according to his glorious power, unto all patience and longsuffering with joyfulness." This "might" and strength is described in Ephesians 1:19-20, "And what is the exceeding greatness of his power to usward who believe, according to the working of his mighty power, which he wrought in Christ, when he raised him from the dead, and set him at his own right hand in the heavenly places." Like Paul prayed for the Spirit's strength, we also should pray that God will strengthen us. The power that is available to us is the same power God used when He raised Jesus from the dead. We must resist sin, but we have God's strength with which to do it.

How do we mortify the deeds of the body? The Bible tells us that we do it "through the Spirit" (v. 13) and that it involves being "led by the Spirit of God" (v. 14). God doesn't leave us to fight the battle alone. As has been said above, the presence of Christ and the Holy Spirit abiding within us mightily strengthens us. Another thing the Holy Spirit does is to open our eyes so that we may see our sins and failures. We should also pray for this. "Search me, O God, and know my heart: try me, and know my thoughts: and see if there be any wicked way in me, and lead me in the way everlasting" (Ps. 139:23-24). Again the Holy Spirit's ministry of leading us is mentioned. The Spirit shows us the right way and motivates us to follow it.

We must also live in dependence on the Spirit of God. We walk by faith (2 Cor. 5:7). The Spirit makes us able to mortify the deeds of the flesh. We depend on Him for that. Much of this dependence on God is done by knowing and trusting His promises in the Word. "Whereby are given unto us exceeding great and precious promises: that by these ye might be partakers of the divine nature, having escaped the corruption that is in the world through lust" (2 Pet. 1:4). One of these promises is in Philippians 2:12-13, "Wherefore, my beloved, as ye have always obeyed, not as in my presence only, but now much more in my absence, work out your own salvation with fear and trembling. For it is God which worketh in you both to will and to do of his good pleasure." To "work out your salvation" does not mean work to get saved. It means work your salvation out into your practical daily living. We work it out in faith that God will work in us.

Jerry Bridges, in *The Pursuit of Holiness* (pp. 78-79), has this to say about dependence on the Holy Spirit:

> We express our dependence on the Holy Spirit for a holy life in two ways. *The first is through a humble and consistent intake of the Scripture.* If we truly desire to live in the realm of the Spirit we must continually feed our minds with His truth. It is hypocritical to pray for victory over our sins yet be careless in our intake of the Word of God. [24]

It is possible, though, to be consistent in our intake of the Word of God without an attitude of dependence on the Holy Spirit (Is. 66:2). We are to come to the Word in a spirit of humility and contrition because we recognize that we are in a battle with sin and that we need the enlightenment of the Holy Spirit in our hearts.

Another way we express our dependence on the Spirit is to pray for holiness. The Apostle Paul prayed continually for the working of God's Spirit in the lives of those to whom he was writing (Eph. 3:16; Col. 1:9-10; 1 Thess. 5:23; 3:12-13).

The second principal is the importance of the mind. Romans 8:5 says, "For they that are after the flesh do mind the things of the flesh; but they that are after the Spirit the things of the Spirit. For to be carnally minded is death; but to be spiritually minded is life and peace." We will be either carnally minded or spiritually minded. Those who are seeking to walk in the Spirit are also seeking to be spiritually minded. What a person is depends largely on what his heart's attitudes are centered on and how he thinks. "For as he thinketh in his heart, so is he" (Prov. 23:7). Jesus said that the greatest commandment was to "love the Lord thy God with all thy heart, and with all thy soul, and with all thy *mind*, and with all thy strength" (Mark 12:30). It is certainly a good idea to pray that you will love God like this.

What is the carnal mind? The Greek word defines carnal as "fleshly." It is a mind controlled by and yielded to the flesh. In verses five through eight, the carnal mind is said to be the enemy of God, it leads to death, it is not subject to the Law of God, it thinks about the things of the world and the flesh, and it cannot please God. The carnal mind is "not subject to the law of God, neither indeed can be" (v. 7). Therefore, those who are unsaved ("in the flesh" v. 8) cannot please God, because they are carnally minded. They cannot be spiritually minded, because they do not have the Spirit of God.

However, Christians (who are "in the spirit"- v. 9) have a choice. They can be carnally minded or spiritually minded. What kind of mind is the spiritual mind? It is a mind that loves God. It is a mind that leads to "life and peace" (v. 6). This mind thinks about the things of God (v. 5). Foremost in those things would be the Word of God. "This book of the law shall not depart out of thy mouth; but thou shalt meditate therein day and night, that thou mayest observe to do according to all that is written therein: for then thou shalt make thy way prosperous, and then thou shalt have good success" (Joshua 1:8). "But his delight is in the law of the LORD; and in his law doth he meditate day and night. And he shall be like a tree planted by the rivers of water, that bringeth forth his fruit in his season; his leaf also shall not wither; and whatsoever he doeth shall prosper" (Ps. 1:2-3). Spiritual prosperity comes from filling your mind with the Word of God. Peace comes from centering your mind on God in faith, which comes from the word of God. "Thou wilt keep him in perfect peace, whose mind is stayed on thee: because he trusteth in thee" and "So then faith cometh by hearing, and hearing by the word of God" (Is. 26:3; Rom. 10:17). The proper attitude is necessary when approaching the Word of God. That attitude consists of an intent to find God's will and do it. "Ezra had prepared his heart to *seek* the law of the LORD, *and to do it*, and to teach in Israel statutes and judgments" (Ezra 7:10; cf. Jm. 1:23). Every Christian should make this an absolute priority. "Man shall not live by bread alone, but by every word that proceedeth out of the mouth of God" (Mt. 4:4). The word guides the opinions and attitudes of a believer's mind. The Word of God transforms and renews the mind (Rom. 12:1-2). A renewed mind transforms the life. As a Christian you are commanded to be "transformed by the renewing of your mind, that ye may prove what is that good, and acceptable, and perfect, will of God" (Rom. 12:2).

The Bible is indispensable in this process and pursuit of sanctification. It is the greatest of the Spirit's tools. The Holy Spirit speaks to us through the Word, but it is our responsibility, with His help and strength, to respond to what we learn there. The ultimate end of all Bible teaching, reading, study, memorizing, and meditation is to apply the Word to our lives so that we may be obedient to it. One of the greatest statements on this in the Bible is from James:

Wherefore lay apart all filthiness and superfluity of naughtiness, and receive with meekness the engrafted word, which is able to save your souls. But be ye doers of the word, and not hearers only, deceiving your own selves. For if any be a hearer of the word, and not a doer, he is like unto a man beholding his natural face in a glass: For he beholdeth himself, and goeth his way, and straightway forgetteth what manner of man he was. But whoso looketh into the perfect law of liberty, and continueth therein, he being not a forgetful hearer, but a doer of the work, this man shall be blessed in his deed. (James 1:21-25)

The third principle is that we have the assurance of our special identity in Christ and of a certain and bright hope for the future. There are three distinct promises and several important truths in Romans 8:10-16. One of these promises is unconditional, but you can only have one of the other two. They are dependent on certain conditions. The first promise is in verse eleven and follows a statement in verse ten that, if the Spirit dwells in you, "the body is dead because of sin." The term "dead" here does not mean fit for the grave. It means ineffective in the sense that we have been freed from its power and it is the equivalent of what we learned in chapter six that the "flesh" no longer dominates and controls a believer. The opposite is also true that if the Spirit dwells in you, there is a holy vibrant life in you. Your body is the subject of the unconditional promise, "if the Spirit of him that raised up Jesus from the dead dwell in you, he that raised up Christ from the dead shall also quicken your mortal bodies by his Spirit that dwelleth in you" (v. 11). This is our hope for the future. One day, we will receive a brand new resurrected body like His body (1 John 3:1-3; Phil. 3:21). The promise is dependent on having the Holy Spirit living in you; a condition that is fulfilled by all who are saved. Knowing that we have the Spirit of life dwelling in us and that this body we sometimes have so much trouble with will be changed into a righteous eternal body like His, we also know that we have no obligation to fulfill the desires and deeds of the flesh (v. 12).

The next two promises (v. 13), are conditioned on how we handle the flesh. If we yield to the lusts of the flesh and commit sin, the result may be severe, even death. "Be not deceived; God is not mocked: for whatsoever a man soweth, that shall he also reap. For he that soweth to his flesh shall of the flesh reap corruption" (Gal. 6:7-8a). However, there is another option that is better. Resist the lusts of the flesh, be obedient to God, and you will live physically and enjoy God's blessings in this life; "but he that soweth to the Spirit shall of the Spirit reap life everlasting. And let us not be weary in well doing: for in due season we shall reap, if we faint not" (Gal. 3:8b-7).

What if you generally follow the Lord, but you fail from time to time? This is an experience we all have. When we fail God by sinning, it breaks our fellowship with God. The answer to forgiveness and restoration to fellowship with God is found in 1 John 1:9. "If we confess our sins, he is faithful and just to forgive us our sins, and to cleanse us from all unrighteousness."

According to verse fourteen, if you walk after the Spirit, you are being led by the Spirit and this is evidence that you are a child of God. In verse 15, the Spirit is called "the Spirit of adoption." This refers back to the resurrection in verse eleven, because the "adoption" is the "redemption of our body" (v. 23). You do not have the actual adoption yet, but you do have the Spirit of Adoption, the Holy Spirit. The Spirit of God will make it clear to you that you are a child of God (v. 16). This is a certain and sure hope.

These promises and assurances are significant for the conflict we have been studying. They can give an encouragement and a strength you would not otherwise have. You know who you are, a child of God and a saint. That cannot be changed. It is sure and certain. You are also given a great and certain hope that one day you will live forever in a pure righteous body free from the very presence of the sin nature and of sinful deeds. Knowing who we are and where we are going imparts a certain confidence to our hearts that helps us face this conflict, realizing that as we do so, God is with us and ultimate victory will be ours.

Fourth, to mortify the deeds of the flesh is a command and a responsibility. It cannot be done without the Spirit's help, but it is our responsibility to do it. Some say, "Let go and let God." However, in this regard, we depend fully on God, but we must face the conflict and fight it. Others say, "Stop trying and start trusting." We must trust, but keep on trying. It is not one or the other. It is both. Someone said to "pray as if it all depends on God, then get up and work as if it all depends on you." It is you who mortifies the deeds of the flesh, but it is done *through the Spirit.* "Mortify therefore your members which are upon the earth; fornication, uncleanness, inordinate affection, evil concupiscence, and covetousness, which is idolatry" (Col. 3:5). "Wherefore seeing we also are compassed about with so great a cloud of witnesses, let us lay aside every weight, and the sin which doth so easily beset us, and let us run with patience the race that is set before us" (Heb. 12:1). This matter of sanctification is a partnership between God and man (Phil. 2:12-13).

The fifth through the seventh principles were suggested by Jerry Bridges.

The fifth principle is to have conviction. We must be convinced that holiness and obedience is necessary and important. We must be convicted that it is God's will for us. "We must believe that the pursuit of holiness is worth the effort and pain required to mortify the misdeeds of the body ... Not only must we develop conviction for living a holy life in general, but we must also develop convictions in specific areas of obedience." [25] This conviction comes from loving God in our hearts. Some people are "lovers of their own selves" (2 Tim. 3:2) and "lovers of pleasures more than lovers of God" (2 Tim. 3:4). We must love God more than pleasure and more than ourselves and more than anything. "He that loveth father or mother more than me is not worthy of me: and he that loveth son or daughter more than me is not worthy of me" (Mt. 10:37).

Jesus said, "He that hath my commandments, and keepeth them, he it is that loveth me" (John 14:21). In order to keep His commandments, we must *know what they are.*
The only way to obtain and know God's will is to learn it from the Bible. This makes it absolutely necessary that every believer have a regular intake of the Scriptures

through hearing them taught, reading them, studying them, memorizing them, and meditating on them. Memorizing is an especially effective way to avoid sin. It was a method used by Jesus, which paid off in Matthew 4 when He was tempted by the Devil. The Bible says, "Wherewithal shall a young man cleanse his way? By taking heed thereto according to thy word. Thy word have I hid in mine heart, that I might not sin against thee" (Ps. 119:9, 11).

The sixth principle to mortify the deeds of the flesh is to have Commitment. "So likewise, whosoever he be of you that forsaketh not all that he hath, he cannot be my disciple" (Luke 14:33). "We must honestly face the question, 'Am I willing to give up a certain habit or practice that is keeping me from holiness?'" [26] Our commitment is to holiness, godliness, and obedience in all areas of our lives and at all times. This attitude will keep us aware of the need to always look closely at our actions and words so that we may always be obedient to the Lord.

The seventh principle is to exercise personal discipline. Discipline or self-control (called "temperance") is a fruit of the Holy Spirit (Gal. 5:22-23). Discipline is also not a word that sits well with many of us. We prefer just a touch of laziness or self-indulgence. Discipline is just hard to do. However, Paul said, "But I keep under my body, and bring it into subjection" 1 Cor. 9:27). Paul also said, "But refuse profane and old wives' fables, and exercise thyself rather unto godliness. For bodily exercise profiteth little: but godliness is profitable unto all things, having promise of the life that now is, and of that which is to come" (1 Tim. 4:6-7). Exercise yourself, train yourself in godliness. These verses do not say that bodily exercise has little profit. Body exercise is of great profit, but godly exercise is of so much more profit that it makes bodily exercise seem to profit little *by comparison*. As time goes on and we grow in Christ, we must develop godly habits of life. Holiness and godliness are not instant attainments in the Christian life. We seek to obey God at all times, but Godly holy habits and character are developed over time. In fact, it takes a lifetime. We have developed many habits of sin in our lives. These must end and be replaced with righteous habits. This certainly requires the strength and power of the Holy Spirit, but it requires conviction, commitment, and discipline on our part, also. It also requires looking to God in faith, because all this conviction, commitment, and discipline is available from the Holy Spirit.

It seems appropriate to end this section with another quote by Jerry Bridges from his book *The Pursuit of Holiness*, page 157.

> God has provided all we need for our pursuit of holiness. He has delivered us from the reign of sin and given us His indwelling Holy Spirit. He has revealed His will for holy living in His Word, and He works in us to will and to act according to His good purpose. He has sent pastors and teachers to exhort and encourage us in the path of holiness; and He answers our prayers when we cry to Him for strength against temptation.
>
> Truly the choice is ours. What will we choose? Will we accept our responsibility and discipline ourselves to live in habitual obedience to the will of God? Will we persevere in the face

of frequent failure, resolving never to give up? Will we decide that personal holiness is worth the price of saying no to our body's demands to indulge its appetites? ...

If you make that decision, you will experience the fullness of joy which Christ has promised to those who walk in obedience to Him. [27]

Chapter Four

The Glorification of Believers
Romans 8:17-39

The last half of chapter eight is filled with references to the future of believers and the world. It starts off in verse seventeen with a declaration that we are heirs of God (vv. 17-18). In spite of the suffering and turmoil in the world, there is hope (vv. 19-25). The hope that God gives involves an ultimate renewal of nature and animals, as well as a new body for Christians like the body of the Lord Jesus Christ. This leads to a discussion of God's purpose and plan for the ultimate destiny of believers (vv. 26-30). Christians are predestined to be conformed to the image of Christ. The section also includes some practical things for our lives now, such as the Holy Spirit praying for us, helping us to pray, and God being at work in all our circumstances. Finally, the chapter ends with an assurance of the love of God as an eternal unchangeable possession (vv. 31-39). We can never be separated from His love. No person or any other creature, which includes each of us, can separate us from His love. What a triumphant cry of victory!

Declared to be Heirs of God
(Romans 8:17-18)

17 ¶And if children, then heirs; heirs of God, and joint-heirs with Christ; if so be that we suffer with him, that we may be also glorified together.
18 For I reckon that the sufferings of this present time are not worthy to be compared with the glory which shall be revealed in us.

As His children, we are heirs of God (v. 17). The Lord Jesus, the only begotten Son of God, has an inheritance from God the Father. We will share in that inheritance and, so, are joint-heirs with Christ. The inheritance is connected with the end of the church age and the beginning of the Millennium, when Christ will reign for one thousand years (Rev. 20:1-6). Christ's inheritance is illustrated in His parable of the nobleman in Luke 19:12-27. A nobleman went into a far country to receive a kingdom, as Christ has now ascended into heaven and is awaiting His second coming. The nobleman returned and received the Kingdom. The Bible tells us that when Christ returns after the Great Tribulation, he will rule the earth (Mt. 24:21; Luke 1:33; Mt. 25:31; 19:15). After the nobleman had become the king, he called his ten servants, to whom he had given ten pounds, when he went into the far country. He judged them as to how well they had traded and gained profit on the money. In our case we will be judged as to how well we have served

Him with the abilities and opportunities He has given us (Rom. 14:10; 1 Cor. 3:11-15; 2 Cor. 5:10). The servant who had gained ten pounds received authority over ten cities. The servant who had gained five pounds received authority over five cities. However, the servant who had been given one pound and had gained none, because he was too timid to try, received no authority and the pound he had was taken and given to him who had gained ten pounds. The servants were granted the privilege of sharing in the inherited kingdom of the nobleman. They became joint-heirs with him. We also will be given the blessing of ruling with Christ in His Millennial Kingdom (Rev. 1:6; 2:27; Rev. 5:10; Rev. 20:1-6).

Verse seventeen adds "if so be that we suffer with him, that we may be also glorified together." The verse seems to be telling us that our inheritance depends on whether we suffer with Christ or not. The phrase "if so be" comes from a Greek word that in other places means "seeing" and "though" in the sense of "since" (2 Thess. 1:6; 1 Cor. 8:5). So, the idea of "if so be" may be a little more certain than it appears at first glance. Regardless of that, however, there is at least one aspect of our inheritance that depends on suffering. "If we suffer, we shall also reign with him: if we deny him, he also will deny us" (2 Tim. 2:12). This verse seems to plainly say that if we deny Christ in our lives here, he will deny us. It is not that He will disown us or deny knowing us. The next verse says that even if we do not believe Him, He will abide faithful. He cannot deny Himself (2 Tim. 2:13) and we are part of Him (Eph. 5:30). So, it must mean that He will deny us the privilege of reigning with Him. I suspect that those of us who do not reign with Him will be priests for Him, since Rev. 5:10 says, "And hast made us unto our God *kings and priests*: and we shall reign on the earth."

Nevertheless, you can be encouraged about this. It is not hard to come by opportunities to suffer with Christ. We do not have to suffer with the same severity Paul did, who was whipped, stoned, starved, imprisoned, shipwrecked, in peril, and in need (2 Cor. 11:23-28). No, the truth is "all that will live godly in Christ Jesus shall suffer persecution" (2 Tim. 3:12). It may only be a sneer here or a snicker there or a snide remark, but it is suffering with Christ. Others may think it strange you do not do what they do and say ugly things about you behind your back (1 Pet. 4:4). In fact, the process of seeking to live godly has its own variety of suffering. Jesus said, "If any man will come after me, let him deny himself, and take up his cross daily, and follow me" (Luke 9:23). Deny yourself; die to yourself. To deny yourself your own pleasure and to discipline your own behavior, doesn't necessarily *feel* good. It hurts sometimes. All you have to do is seek to obey God with all your heart and you will suffer.

There are things that await us that are unconditional. First, we will have a new body that is like the Lord's body. Philippians 3:20-21 describes this new body, "For our conversation is in heaven; from whence also we look for the Saviour, the Lord Jesus Christ: Who shall change our vile body, that it may be fashioned like unto his glorious body, according to the working whereby he is able even to subdue all things unto himself." His body could eat but did not need to (John 21:9-12), was heavenly flesh (1 Cor. 15:39-49), would never die, was forever perfectly healthy, youthful, energetic (1 Cor. 15:42-43), could pass through walls (John 20:19, 26), and could appear or disappear at will (Luke 24:31) yet it was a physical body, a body of flesh (1 Cor. 15:39-41). We all will have this type of body. When we get this body, it is referred to as the "redemption of the body" (Rom. 8:23) and the "redemption of the purchased possession" (Eph. 1:14).

Jesus also promised us, "In my Father's house are many mansions: if it were not so, I would have told you. I go to prepare a place for you" (John 14:2). The Lord has prepared a home in heaven for us. Our homes are in God's city, New Jerusalem, near the throne of God. New Jerusalem is described in Revelation twenty-one. Its size has been estimated at fifteen hundred miles in length and breadth and height. It will have a wall with foundations made of precious jewels, twelve gates of pearl, and a street of pure gold (Rev. 21:12-21). It is a glorious bright happy place of no death, sorrow, tears, pain, or disease (Rev. 21:4). We will have a new body, a new home, and riches built up by our years of serving the Lord (Mt. 6:19-21). We have much to look forward to, much awaiting us beyond this life. Remember:

> *If ye then be risen with Christ, seek those things which are above, where Christ sitteth on the right hand of God. Set your affection on things above, not on things on the earth. For ye are dead, and your life is hid with Christ in God. When Christ, who is our life, shall appear, then shall ye also appear with him in glory.*
> (Col. 3:1-4).

"For I reckon that the sufferings of this present time are not worthy to be compared with the glory which shall be revealed in us" (Rom. 8:17). Suffering takes on a whole new perspective when viewed in comparison to what God has for us in the future. The future will be glorious for all of us, without exception. God has great beauty, happiness, and wonder in store for us. There will also be great glory revealed through us. We will be the display of the glory of God's grace (Eph. 1:6, 12, 14). The wonder and beauty of what God has done for us, all those things described in Romans 1:1-8:16, will be seen and glory will be given to God. We, new creatures in Christ created for God's glory (2 Cor. 5:17; 1 Cor. 10:31), will be able to glorify Him throughout eternity. In 2011, I lost a colleague and friend to complications of cancer. The day he died he told a mutual friend of ours, "This is what I've lived my whole life for!"

Delivered By Hope
Romans 8:19-25

19 For the earnest expectation of the creature waiteth for the manifestation of the sons of God.
20 For the creature was made subject to vanity, not willingly, but by reason of him who hath subjected the same in hope,
21 Because the creature itself also shall be delivered from the bondage of corruption into the glorious liberty of the children of God.
22 For we know that the whole creation groaneth and travaileth in pain together until now.
23 And not only they, but ourselves also, which have the

firstfruits of the Spirit, even we ourselves groan within ourselves, waiting for the adoption, to wit, the redemption of our body.
24 For we are saved by hope: but hope that is seen is not hope: for what a man seeth, why doth he yet hope for?
25 But if we hope for that we see not, then do we with patience wait for it.

It is clear from verse nineteen through twenty-two that nature itself will be rejuvenated when Christ comes again. When sin came into the world through Adam, it drastically affected all of nature. At that time, God told Adam that "cursed is the ground for thy sake; in sorrow shalt thou eat of it all the days of thy life; thorns also and thistles shall it bring forth to thee; and thou shalt eat the herb of the field; in the sweat of thy face shalt thou eat bread" (Gen. 3:17-19). Death not only came upon all people, but it came upon all animals too. Before Adam, there was no death.

During the Millennium, there will be a great change to nature. In his book, *Things to Come*, J. Dwight Pentecost described some of the conditions prevailing in the Millennium. The curse on the earth spoken of in Genesis three will be removed. The earth will produce more abundance of crops than today (Amos 9:13) and be more like a garden (Is. 29:17; 35:7). The ferociousness of animals will cease (Is. 11:6-9; 35:9; 65:25). Sickness will be taken away (Is. 33:24; Jer. 30:17; Ezek. 34:16). Deformities will be healed (Is. 29:18-19; 35:3-6). There will even be a restoration of long lives (Is. 65:20). There will be an increase of light from the sun and moon (Is. 30:26). This is perhaps the reason for the longer and more abundant growing seasons. [28]

Verse twenty-three, "not only they, but ourselves also," shows that there is a longing in believers to participate in what God will do during that time. It has a special application to us that goes beyond the things mentioned in the last paragraph. It has to do with the "redemption of our body." That new body has been described above. The redemption is connected with the "adoption." The verse tells us "we ourselves groan within ourselves, waiting for the adoption, to wit, the redemption of our body." The fact that we are "waiting" for the adoption makes it clear that we *do not yet have* the adoption. It is still future, even though we have the "spirit of adoption" at the present time (Rom. 8:15). The adoption is said to *be* the redemption of our bodies. It is something God has planned for us, designed us for, and determined to give us.

All of these things are details of our hope (vv. 24-25). Hope saves us; therefore hope is faith, since we are also saved through faith. Hope is viewed as something that is certain, not something that we wish for, but may or may not happen. Our hope is centered in "that blessed hope, and the glorious appearing of the great God and our Saviour Jesus Christ" (Titus 2:13). All the glorious things coming in the future spring from that one event, the coming of Christ. So, our hope in the future is sure and certain. It will truly be a final and complete salvation from the very presence of sin. There will be no more sin nature with which to battle. There will be no more warfare within ourselves. We have peace with God and, with no more conflict in our souls, we will have perfect peace within forever. Hope is also centered on things we do not yet see. Our future is something we see only by the eyes of faith. It is something worth waiting for and we must do so with patience.

Destined to God's Purpose
Romans 8:26-30

26 ¶Likewise the Spirit also helpeth our infirmities: for we know not what we should pray for as we ought: but the Spirit itself maketh intercession for us with groanings which cannot be uttered.
27 And he that searcheth the hearts knoweth what is the mind of the Spirit, because he maketh intercession for the saints according to the will of God.
28 And we know that all things work together for good to them that love God, to them who are the called according to his purpose.
29 ¶For whom he did foreknow, he also did predestinate to be conformed to the image of his Son, that he might be the firstborn among many brethren.
30 Moreover whom he did predestinate, them he also called: and whom he called, them he also justified: and whom he justified, them he also glorified.

There have been volumes written about this portion of Scripture. Nevertheless, I will try to summarize the major points in a few words. Verses twenty-six and twenty-seven show us how the Spirit helps our prayer life. Then verse twenty-eight says that everything works together for our good. This is followed by the fact that we are predestinated to be conformed to the image of Christ. That is why all things work together for our good.

Romans 8:26-28 has some very practical truths that stand out. First, we have a problem. We often do not know what we should request from God. Experience shows that our prayers can become habitual, repetitive, and stiff. Instead of praying for real needs, we can let our requests be for the same general things each time and miss some real needs. To help in this, the Spirit, who always knows exactly what to pray for, "makes intercession for us." He does this with "groaning which cannot be uttered." The Spirit does not just guide our prayers so that we pray for the right things. He prays for us. Since it is in groaning that *cannot be uttered,* it is not us praying. The Spirit is making requests that we cannot hear. This is a great help and blessing, because we know that our true needs are being placed before our heavenly Father and that every request is according to His will.

This by itself can explain Romans 8:28. One reason we can know that everything that happens works together for our good, is because the Spirit is praying for us. Notice verse twenty-eight says "all things" work together for good. Take this at face value. Believe what it says. Everything that happens to you is designed to produce good in your life. God is in control. If God allows something to happen, look for the good in it. The circumstances may hurt, but it is still good. This is why the Lord tells us to give "thanks always *for all things* unto God" (Eph. 5:20) and, "*In everything* give thanks: for this is the will of God in Christ Jesus concerning you" (1 Thess. 5:18). We are to thank God "in" everything and "for" everything."

This promise of verse twenty-eight is made to those who love God. Remember that those who love God are those who keep His commandments (John 14:21; 1 John 5:3). There are similar promises made in the Scriptures about how God guides His followers. "The steps of a good man are ordered by the LORD: and he delighteth in his way" (Ps. 37:23). "A man's heart deviseth his way: but the LORD directeth his steps" (Prov. 16:9). If we do not keep God's commands the Lord will likely bring circumstances into our lives that are nothing more than a good old fashioned whipping (Heb. 12:4-13). Even whippings are cause for thanksgiving to God. If God loves us enough to correct us (and we all need it from time to time), we should thank God for what He has brought into our lives to straighten us out. However, do not think that difficult circumstances are always the result of sin. Sometimes hard and difficult times come to teach us valuable lessons and to mold our character (1 Peter 1:6-8). Remember, "There hath no temptation (includes trials) taken you but such as is common to man: but God *is* faithful, who will not suffer you to be tempted above that ye are able; but will with the temptation also make a way to escape, that ye may be able to bear *it*."

There is a deeper reason for all things working together for good in verse twenty-eight. This promise is also directed "to them who are the called according to his purpose." This includes every Christian. We have all been called according to His purpose. In this context, the purpose of God is explained in Romans 8:29-30, "For whom he did foreknow, he also did predestinate to be conformed to the image of his Son, that he might be the firstborn among many brethren. Moreover whom he did predestinate, them he also called: and whom he called, them he also justified: and whom he justified, them he also glorified." The purpose is that Christ may be the first-born of many brethren who bear His image. That is, we are all predestined to be conformed to His image. It is also called the glorification of the Christian (v. 30). The image we will bear will be physical, because we will have a body like His, as we have previously seen. But, there will be much more to it. When the Bible says we will be "like" Him (1 John 3:1-3), it goes much deeper than an outer image. We will also bear His character. Eph. 1:4 says that "he hath chosen us in him before the foundation of the world, that we should be holy and without blame before him in love." God has chosen us for the purpose of making us "holy and without blame." Jesus further says that when He died for the church, He did it so "That he might sanctify and cleanse it with the washing of water by the word, that he might present it to himself a glorious church, not having spot, or wrinkle, or any such thing; but that it should be holy and without blemish" (Eph. 5:26-27). When the day comes for us to be presented to Him, He wants us in this condition. It is tied to the process of sanctification which is operating in this life with a goal of ultimately arriving at total holiness. That is why the prayer help of the Holy Spirit and the guidance and directing work of God in our lives is so vital.

We cannot pass over this passage without a closer look at *predestination*. The word means to *appoint beforehand* or *to determine beforehand*. There are several other things mentioned in regard to predestination: foreknowledge, calling, justification, and glorification. These are placed in a specific order of occurrence. It starts with foreknowledge, then predestination, followed by calling, next justification, and finally glorification. Which of these items is the object of predestination? Is the elect Christian predestined to justification? No, he is predestinated to glorification, nothing more. The same is true with election or choosing in Ephesians 1:4. Christians were chosen in Christ before the foundation of the world, not to salvation, but *to be holy and without blame before Him in love.* Both election and predestination are focused on the end of the Christian life, *not the beginning.*

It is clear that foreknowledge plays a prominent part in predestination as it does in election; "Elect *according to the foreknowledge* of God the Father, through sanctification of the Spirit" (1 Peter 1:2). In fact, the wording of the passages is that God's acts of predestination and election were *based and founded* on His foreknowledge. It was *those He foreknew that He predestinated.* The word "foreknowledge" comes from the Greek word *proginōskō* and means "to have knowledge before hand." [29] However, Romans 8:29-30 does not tell us what God foreknew. Perhaps the context can tell us more. God knows all things before they happen. He is *all knowing.* Foreknowledge is not something God *does.* It is part of what *He is.* It is one of His characteristics. It should be obvious that God knows all about each of us. He knew all about each of us before we were born, even before He created human beings. So, applying this to the context, He clearly knew, before He did any predestinating at all, who He would call and who, responding with faith, He would justify. Those are the ones He predestinated to be conformed to the image of His Son, to be glorified. My commentary on Ephesians has a whole chapter on the subject of election and predestination based on Ephesians 1:4. I have included and expanded that chapter in this volume as an *Afterwards* to give the reader fuller information and not leave them confused.

God's Domain of Love
Romans 8:31-39

31 ¶What shall we then say to these things? If God be for us, who can be against us?
32 He that spared not his own Son, but delivered him up for us all, how shall he not with him also freely give us all things?
33 Who shall lay any thing to the charge of God's elect? It is God that justifieth.
34 Who is he that condemneth? It is Christ that died, yea rather, that is risen again, who is even at the right hand of God, who also maketh intercession for us.
35 Who shall separate us from the love of Christ? shall tribulation, or distress, or persecution, or famine, or nakedness, or peril, or sword?
36 As it is written, For thy sake we are killed all the day long; we are accounted as sheep for the slaughter.
37 Nay, in all these things we are more than conquerors through him that loved us.
38 For I am persuaded, that neither death, nor life, nor angels, nor principalities, nor powers, nor things present, nor things to come,
39 Nor height, nor depth, nor any other creature, shall be able to separate us from the love of God, which is in Christ Jesus our Lord.

This passage is one of the greatest and most encouraging in the Word of God. If anyone needs proof of eternal security, that once we are saved we will always be saved, they will find it in this passage. We are settled, secure, and firmly planted in the love of God. Looking back over all that we have covered in the previous parts of the Book of Romans, we have to exclaim, "How great is the love of God!"

This entire passage is written to explain the statement, "If God be for us, who can be against us" (Rom. 8:31)? To reinforce this, He makes the following points.

1) Our place in the love of God is firmly founded on the fact that God gave His Son for us and will freely give us whatever we need (v. 32).

2) No one can condemn us (not man, Satan, or angels). Christ died for us, rose again, and we are justified (v. 33, 34).

3) Christ makes intercession for us. He sits at the right hand of God and has the Father's ear (v. 34). God will *always* answer His prayers.

4) Nothing can separate us from the love of God (vv. 35-39)

    a) That includes any kind of distress or trouble. We are more than conquerors through Him (vv. 35-37).

    b) Nothing else we could ever encounter can separate us from the love of God. This includes life and death, things present, and things to come (vv. 38-39).

In other words, now that we are justified, sanctified, and in Christ NOHING will ever separate us from the love of God in Christ Jesus. No matter what wiles of the Devil are unleashed against us, we are secure. No matter what are our failures, we are secure in Him. No matter what circumstances we face, we are secure in Him. We are eternally secure in Him!

Chapter Five

The Confirmation of the Promises to Israel
Romans 9:1-11:36

At this point, we will travel in a different direction. The underlying question of Romans 9-11 is, "What is Israel's place in this new arrangement that was initiated by the crucifixion and resurrection of the Lord?" It's a necessary question, because the Jews thought they were the center of the universe as far as God is concerned. The Gentiles did not matter. To them, the Gentiles were spiritually unclean and unworthy of God's blessings. What God is about to do in chapter nine is to let them know that He chose them for His own reasons, not because of any good he found in them. He chose the nation of Israel by grace. If He can do that to the Jews, He can also include the Gentiles in His grace.

Introduction to the Jews
Romans 9:1-8

1 ¶I say the truth in Christ, I lie not, my conscience also bearing me witness in the Holy Ghost,
2 That I have great heaviness and continual sorrow in my heart.
3 For I could wish that myself were accursed from Christ for my brethren, my kinsmen according to the flesh
(Rom. 9:1-3).

The section starts off with a small introduction to the Jews (Rom. 9:1-8) and of Paul's sorrow at their general rejection of the gospel. He had a great burden for the Jews, describing his sorrow as "continual" and "heaviness." If it were possible, Paul could have wished to go to Hell in their stead, in their place. But it was not possible.

> *4 Who are Israelites; to whom pertaineth the adoption, and the glory, and the covenants, and the giving of the law, and the service of God, and the promises;*
> *5 Whose are the fathers, and of whom as concerning the flesh Christ came, who is over all, God blessed for ever. Amen.*
> (Rom. 9:4-5)

There are several things listed that can be called blessings to the Jews (vv. 4-5). Let's define each one:
1) The adoption: God considered Israel to be His son and the people of Israel to be his children (Deut. 32:6; Is.

1:2; Hos. 11:1). This is not the new birth given to the church. Nor is it the adoption given to the church and described in Romans 8 as "the redemption of the body." It is God's acceptance and embracing of Israel in a special relationship to Him in which He calls them His children.

2) The glory: God, Himself, is the glory of Israel and He showed up at times in glory, such as, the pillar of fire (Ex. 13:21; 2 Chron. 5:11-14).

3) The covenants: God made covenants with Israel, such as, the Abrahamic Covenant (Gen. 12:1-3), the Mosaic Covenant (Ex. 20:1-26; Ex. 21:1-24:18; Ex. 25:1-40:38), the Davidic Covenant (2 Sam. 7:4-17), the Palestinian Covenant (Deut. 30:1-10), and the New Covenant (Jer. 31:31; Heb. 8:8-14; 12:24). [30]

4) The giving of the Law: This pertains to the giving of the Law of Moses beginning in Ex. 20:1-24.

5) The service of God: This refers to the ceremonial Law of Israel, the tabernacle, and the temple (Ex. 25:1-40:38; the Book of Leviticus).

6) The promises: God gave Israel many special promises beginning with those given to Abraham in Genesis 12:1-3.

7) The fathers: Israel was descended from Abraham, Isaac, and Jacob.

Earlier Paul said that Israel was blessed because God gave the Scriptures of the Old Testament through them (Rom. 3:1-3). Here (v. 5) he lists their greatest blessing. It was through the nation of Israel that Christ came. However, he goes on to say that a true Jew is not one who is merely a descendant of Abraham, Isaac, and Jacob; but he is also a Jew inwardly by faith.

> 6 ¶*Not as though the word of God hath taken none effect. For they are not all Israel, which are of Israel:*
> 7 *Neither, because they are the seed of Abraham, are they all children: but, In Isaac shall thy seed be called.*
> 8 *That is, They which are the children of the flesh, these are not the children of God: but the children of the promise are counted for the seed.*
> (Rom. 9:6-7)

"In Isaac shall thy seed be called" (Rom. 9:7; Gen. 21:12). Isaac was given to Abraham by promise, not by the works of the law (Gal. 4:21-28). We saved Jews and gentiles are the spiritual seed of Abraham. A Jew is the physical seed of Abraham, but a Jew who is a Jew physically only is not a child of God. One who is a Jew both physically and spiritually through faith in Christ are the true heirs of the promises of God to Israel. God has not cast off His chosen nation, as we shall see. God always has a saved remnant of His chosen nation and some day the entire nation will be restored.

According to William MacDonald and Arthur Farstad, in their commentary, *Believer's Bible Commentary: Old and New Testaments*, Romans 9-11 can be simply outlined according to each time period of Israel's existence:

> Israel's Past (Chapter 9)
> Israel's Present (Chapter 10)
> Israel's Future (Chapter 11) [31]

Israel's Past
Romans 9:9-33

The rest of the chapter follows the principle that the true children of Abraham are the children of promise and, therefore, children of God's free grace. God does it this way so that His choice of men or nations will be based on His own mercy, not on their goodness or good works. The reason the choice is by promise is based on a principle. The principle involved is stated several times. For example, Romans 9:11 says, "that the purpose of God according to election might stand, not of works, but of him that calleth." Later it is said, "I will have mercy on whom I will have mercy, and I will have compassion on whom I will have compassion" (Rom. 9:15). Finally, the statement is: "Therefore hath he mercy on whom he will have mercy, and whom he will he hardeneth" (Rom. 9:18) and "Hath not the potter power over the clay, of the same lump to make one vessel unto honour, and another unto dishonor" (Rom. 9:21)?

To explain these statements, God presents three major illustrations (Jacob, Esau, and Pharaoh), explains His status as a potter, gives numerous Scripture references, and deals with certain objections.

This chapter has been called "Righteousness Exemplified in Divine Sovereignty." [32] The emphasis has been on Sovereignty, by which the commentators seem to mean "God is all powerful and does whatever He pleases." The emphasis of the commentators is on the sovereignty of God to the exclusion of His other traits, such as, mercy and grace. While there is some truth in this definition and chapter 9 does show that God's plans are according to the good pleasure of His will (Eph. 1:5, 9), this chapter emphasizes God's mercy, grace, and justice more than His sovereignty . After all, God is trying to show that His choice is a based on mercy and grace. That's what the promise of verses 5-8 is all about. The illustration of His rejection of Pharaoh is a matter of justice and glory, as we shall see.

The first illustration: Jacob and Esau (Rom. 9:9-16)

9 For this is the word of promise, At this time will I come, and Sara shall have a son.
10 And not only this; but when Rebecca also had conceived by one, even by our father Isaac;
11 (For the children being not yet born, neither having done any good or evil, that the purpose of God according to election might stand, not of works, but of him that calleth;)
12 It was said unto her, The elder shall serve the younger.
13 As it is written, Jacob have I loved, but Esau have I hated.
14 ¶What shall we say then? Is there unrighteousness with God? God forbid.
15 For he saith to Moses, I will have mercy on whom I will have mercy, and I will have compassion on whom I will have compassion.
16 So then it is not of him that willeth, nor of him that runneth, but of God that sheweth mercy.

The promise that Sarah shall have a son in verse 9 and 12 is mentioned first. The promise was given in Genesis 18:14 and was fulfilled in Genesis 21:1-7, when Isaac was born. Second, verse 12 says that "the elder shall serve the younger." This statement skips ahead several years. Sarah had died and Abraham's servant had gone to Padan-Aram and brought a wife, Rebekah, home for Isaac (Gen. 24). Rebekah became pregnant with twins. Esau was born first and Jacob was born second. Normally the elder would become head of the household and receive the bulk of the inherited goods. Additionally, he would inherit the Abrahamic Covenant. However, God did not let this happen. He chose the younger, Jacob, to be the heir. God loved Jacob in the sense that He favored him. God hated Esau in the sense that He deprived him of the inheritance. The conclusion (vv. 14-16) is: "I will have mercy on whom I will have mercy, and I will have compassion on whom I will have compassion. So then it is not of him that willeth, nor of him that runneth, but of God that sheweth mercy." God doesn't make His plans based on what you or I do, think, say, or want. He made this plan based partly on His mercy and compassion and partly on His wisdom and foreknowledge. Therefore, God's choice of Israel as His chosen people was a matter of mercy. It is clear that this was God's program and the choice was His alone.

The reader should note something very closely here. The above illustration has nothing to do with God's choice of an individual for salvation. It has nothing to do with the basis for individual spiritual election to salvation. The subject is the selection of the head of a new nation. In this case, Jacob was chosen before he was born to show that he was God's choice without any considerations of whether he was a moral man or had any good character. Regardless of the fact that God's choice of us is also a matter of His grace, the subject is still the origin of a nation, not salvation. The Jews were trying to establish their own personal righteousness before God (Rom. 10:1-4) based on their own relationship to the Law. God wants them to know that He didn't choose the Jews because of their works, but rather because of His grace. Their conclusion ought to be that they should come to God for his salvation trusting His grace, not their own righteous works.

The Second Illustration: Pharaoh, King of Egypt
Time of the Exodus
(Rom. 9:17-19)

17 For the scripture saith unto Pharaoh, Even for this same purpose have I raised thee up, that I might shew my power in thee, and that my name might be declared throughout all the earth.
18 Therefore hath he mercy on whom he will have mercy, and whom he will he hardeneth.
19 Thou wilt say then unto me, Why doth he yet find fault? For who hath resisted his will?

These verses refer to the incident of the Exodus, described in the Book of Exodus 1-19. Moses, who was born of the Israelite people, of the tribe of Levy, was called by God to deliver the people of Israel from slavery in Egypt. During the course of the events that followed, Pharaoh, king of Egypt, was repeatedly called upon to release Israel. He refused to do so. Romans 9: 17-18, explains the spiritual realities going on both in God's mind and in Pharaoh's heart. God hardened the heart of Pharaoh so that he would not let the people of Israel go. God used this to refusal to show His great power over Pharaoh and over the god's of Egypt. He used it as an opportunity to spread His glory to other nations.

It is easy for us to understand how God would choose between two babies like Jacob and Esau, especially since the choice was about who would head a nation and not about eternal salvation. However, it is harder to understand this illustration about God hardening the heart of a grown man, especially since it involves a moral and spiritual choice. It is not entirely about the personal spiritual condition of Pharaoh, though. It is about how God dealt with the slave master of the nation of Israel and how He delivered them from this bondage. The hardening of Pharaoh's heart allowed God to bring righteous judgment down on the gods of Egypt, upon the people of Egypt, and upon Pharaoh for their previous sins and idolatry. This resulted in the deliverance of Israel, righteous judgment administered, and God being glorified.

So, what happened to Pharaoh? God hardened his heart, causing him to refuse to free Israel from their slavery. Therefore, God punished him and Egypt with plagues. Is this right? God hardened his heart so he would do wrong and God punished him for doing wrong? That is right. "Therefore hath he mercy on whom he will have mercy, and whom he will he hardeneth" (Rom. 9:18). God anticipated the objection to this. "Why doth he yet find fault? For who hath resisted his will" (Rom. 9:19)? If I'm only doing this sin because God hardened my heart and caused me to do it, I'm not really resisting His will and I'm not responsible. God is! That is the objection.

The Objection Answered:
The Illustration of the Potter
(Rom. 9:20-24)

20 Nay but, O man, who art thou that repliest against God? Shall the thing formed say to him that formed it, Why hast thou made me thus?
21 Hath not the potter power over the clay, of the same lump to make one vessel unto honour, and another unto dishonour?
22 What if God, willing to shew his wrath, and to make his power known, endured with much longsuffering the vessels of wrath fitted to destruction:
23 And that he might make known the riches of his glory on the vessels of mercy, which he had afore prepared unto glory,
24 Even us, whom he hath called, not of the Jews only, but also of the Gentiles?

God has a right to make His creatures into anything He wishes. This only stands to reason, because God is our creator. He has power over us and He owns us, by right of creation. He is God after all and we are only His creatures. Not only that, but we are sinners by choice and God is righteous to punish us for it. The vessels spoken of are people. Clearly there are some people who are "fitted" for destruction. Others are prepared for "glory."

Verse 23 says the vessels of mercy were prepared "afore." Before what? Or, when? Notice what is *not* said. The verses do not say any of the vessels were prepared in eternity past. The "afore" of verse 23 could refer to anytime before God had mercy on them. It could refer to time as well as eternity.

A favorite teaching of the Calvinistic theology that came out of the reformation (1500 AD to 1700 AD) is that "all of God decrees are eternal." According to theologians, a decree is the "predetermined purpose of God" [33] and all of God's decrees were determined in eternity past before creation. Unfortunately, theology is not always in agreement with the Bible and theologians do not always submit their intellect to the Word of God. Such is the case with the term "decree."

The Hebrew word translated "decree" is *choq*. It means, "statute, ordinance, limit, something prescribed, due." [34] In the King James Version, the word is translated decree, ordinance, laws, custom, etc. The use of the word as "decree" is not limited to eternity past. Psalm 148:6 says, "He hath also stablished them for ever and ever: he hath made a decree which shall not pass." In this verse, God is talking about the sun, moon, stars, and other things made during the creation week. The decree itself is not timed. That is God could have declared it before creation or during creation. There is no necessity that it be before creation. Proverbs 8:29 tells us, "When he gave to the sea his decree, that the waters should not pass his commandment: when he appointed the foundations of the earth." In this case the decree is given to the sea, which has already been created. Therefore, here is a decree clearly given in time. Another example is from Jeremiah 5:22, "Fear ye not me? saith the LORD: will ye not tremble at my presence, which have placed the sand for the bound of the sea by a perpetual decree, that it cannot pass it: and though the waves thereof toss themselves, yet can they not prevail; though they roar, yet can they not pass over it?" We have this decree recorded in Genesis 1:9, "And God said, Let the waters under the heaven be gathered together unto one place, and let the dry land appear: and it was so." It is readily acknowledged that God had all His plans in mind before creation by virtue of the fact that He is all-knowing and all-wise. However, a decree seems to be something that is *declared* and made known. Not all of God's decrees were declared in eternity past.

The point of all this is that the use of the term "afore" in Romans 9:23, does *not* automatically apply to eternity past. Many theologians say that in eternity past, God's decrees included *unconditional election*; that a few will be saved and the rest will be damned. To put it another way, some were declared to be vessels of mercy, but most were declared to be vessels of wrath and destruction. Therefore, the reference to these vessels in Romans 9:23 is a reference to this decree. Unconditional election is *never* stated in Scripture. Romans 9 definitely does not state these things.

To risk getting ahead of ourselves, it is very important for the overall argument that the readers of Romans acknowledge God's prerogatives. God made His own choice of Israel to be His people. He did this for His own reasons, not because Israel deserved it. If this can be understood now, later they will accept God's choice to bring the Gentiles to salvation along with the Jews.

How do these principles look in the reality of the actual occurrence? The confrontation with Pharaoh took place in Exodus 5:1 through 14:31. God told Moses He would harden Pharaoh's heart in Exodus 4:21 and in 7:3. The reason was that He might "multiply my signs and my wonders in the land of Egypt." The first time God hardened Pharaoh's heart was Exodus 7:13, three chapters after He first promised it. This was also the first time Moses and Aaron showed Pharaoh the signs God gave them. However, this was not the first time they asked Pharaoh to let Israel go. That happened in Exodus 5:1-4. In that instance, God *did not harden* Pharaoh's heart. Nevertheless, Pharaoh's heart was hard. His answer to Moses and Aaron was, "Who is the LORD, that I should obey his voice to let Israel go? I know not the LORD, neither will I let Israel go" (Ex. 5:2). He followed this up by increasing Israel's burden of brick making. Obviously, Pharaoh's heart was already in a rebellious and wicked condition and God knew it. He refused to acknowledge God or obey Him. God offered Pharaoh a chance to do what was right *before* He hardened Pharaoh's heart, but he refused. *Pharaoh hardened his own heart*, before God ever took the first step to harden him. *After* the incident in Exodus five, God reaffirmed his promise to harden Pharaoh's heart (Ex. 7:3). From Pharaoh's failure to listen to God in Exodus five on there was little left for Pharaoh except judgment. God judged him *by* hardening his heart.

After God hardened Pharaoh in chapter seven, there was a pattern that emerged. In Exodus 7:13, the Lord hardened Pharaoh's heart, but in the next plague, the judgment on the Nile River, it simply says "Pharaoh's heart was hardened" (Ex. 7:22). However, in the plague of the frogs, the story clearly says that Pharaoh *hardened his own heart* (Ex. 8:15). In the next plague of the lice, it is again said simply, "Pharaoh's heart was hardened" (Ex. 8:19). Then, after Moses had removed the next plague of the flies, Pharaoh *once again hardened his own heart*. The death of the cattle found Pharaoh's heart hardened (Ex. 9:7). There is no further mention of God hardening Pharaoh's heart until the plague of boils, when God clearly hardened Pharaoh's heart (Ex. 9:12). The next plague, that of the hail, was one of the worst and yet, once again, Pharaoh *hardened his own heart* (Ex. 9:34). Exodus 10:1 says the Lord hardened the hearts of Pharaoh and his servants so that the Lord could show His signs in Egypt (Ex. 10:1). God was using this opportunity to show the nations His greatness and power and judgment. From this point on, it was the Lord that firmly hardened Pharaoh's heart and finally led him to judgment in the Red Sea (Ex. 10:20; 10:27; 11:10; 14:4, 8, 17; Ps. 136:15). However, God gave Pharaoh many opportunities to submit to Him, without any hardening from God. Nevertheless, Pharaoh refused and hardened his own heart numerous times.

It seems that God gave Pharaoh a chance for mercy. In Exodus five and each time he hardened his own heart, Pharaoh could have repented. According to the established pattern of Scripture, it would seem that if Pharaoh would have repented, he would have been forgiven. This pattern of sin-judgment-repentance-restoration is seen over and over in the Word of God. It is especially evident in the Book of Judges. In 1 Kings 22:1-39, God sent a lying spirit into the false prophets of Ahab, King of Israel. The purpose was to persuade him to go up to Ramoth in Gilead to battle and die. God had judged and condemned him. Prior to this, though, there were many years of rebellion against God and sin in

Ahab's life. God had sent him many warnings through the prophet Elijah, but he ignored them and rebelled against all God said to him. God always seems to give a man a chance to repent before judging him. In 2 Thessalonians 2, there is a huge group of people to whom "God shall send ... strong delusion, that they should believe a lie" (2 Thess. 2:11) that "they all might be damned **who believed not the truth**, but had pleasure in unrighteousness" (2 Thess. 2:12). God Himself will send the strong delusion! However, this is not what some people describe as a "sovereign act," that is, an act of God by the pleasure of His own will without reference to what people do or want. This is a sovereign act of judgment that is solidly based on something men did-refusal to believe the truth. The work with Pharaoh and Egypt fall into the same category.

The point of Romans 9:1-21 is that God, as creator has the right to deal with people in whatever way He chooses. He has the right to bless them or curse them. He has the right to judge them or to be gracious to them. This is exactly what He did with Israel, He chose Israel for His own reasons, not because they earned it. He chose Israel because He loved Abraham, Isaac, and Jacob and because He loved the nation (Deut. 4:37; 7:7-8).

God's Right to Bless the Gentiles
(Rom. 9:25-29)

25 ¶*As he saith also in Osee, I will call them my people, which were not my people; and her beloved, which was not beloved.*
26 *And it shall come to pass, that in the place where it was*

said unto them, Ye are not my people; there shall they be called the children of the living God.
27 Esaias also crieth concerning Israel, Though the number of the children of Israel be as the sand of the sea, a remnant shall be saved:
28 For he will finish the work, and cut it short in righteousness: because a short work will the Lord make upon the earth.
29 And as Esaias said before, Except the Lord of Sabaoth had left us a seed, we had been as Sodoma, and been made like unto Gomorrha.

If God has the right to bless Israel, He also has the right to bless the Gentiles (Romans 9:22-24). That is exactly what He has done as Paul explains in Romans 9:25-29.

Paul bases the statement that the Gentiles will be God's people (v. 25) on Hos. 2:23. Jameson, Fausett, and Brown say that this is a "passage relating immediately, not to the heathen, but to the kingdom of the ten tribes; but since they had sunk to the level of the heathen, who were 'not God's people,' and in that sense 'not beloved,' the apostle legitimately applies it to the heathen." [35] So, God will include Gentiles among His people. He will extend to them the blessings of salvation. As the Lord says in Ephesians 2:11-13: "Wherefore remember, that ye being in time past Gentiles ... That at that time ye were without Christ, being aliens from the commonwealth of Israel, and strangers from the covenants of promise, having no hope, and without God in the world: But now in Christ Jesus ye who sometimes were far off are made nigh by the blood of Christ."

So where does that leave Israel? Paul quotes from Isaiah 22:22-23 to make the point that not all the physical descendants of Jacob will be saved. Even if the physical descendants of Israel are as numerous as the sand grains on the beaches of the world, only a small number will be saved (vv. 27-29). This is because the Jews must come to God in the same way as the Gentiles, through faith in the Lord Jesus Christ. Most of the Jews will reject this, because they do not believe that Jesus is their Messiah.

A Stone of Stumbling
(Rom. 9:30-33)

30 ¶*What shall we say then? That the Gentiles, which followed not after righteousness, have attained to righteousness, even the righteousness which is of faith.*
31 *But Israel, which followed after the law of righteousness, hath not attained to the law of righteousness.*
32 *Wherefore? Because they sought it not by faith, but as it were by the works of the law. For they stumbled at that stumblingstone;*
33 *As it is written, Behold, I lay in Sion a stumblingstone and rock of offence: and whosoever believeth on him shall not be ashamed.*

The first conclusion is that many of the Gentiles have been glad to embrace the righteousness of God (justification) that comes through faith in Christ (v. 30). They have learned that they cannot be righteous through personal effort in keeping the law. However, Israel has failed to obtain righteousness by keeping the law, even though they sought it (v. 31). Why did they not find the righteousness that is by faith? They sought to present their own righteousness to God and it simply wasn't good enough (See Rom. 3; Is. 64:6). They just cannot understand how any righteousness could be counted to a person unless it comes through much effort to keep the Law (v. 32). They cannot grasp the concept of grace.

It was Jesus Christ who came to make the way to obtain righteousness through faith. Since the Jews could not understand this, he became a "stone of stumbling and rock of offense." Basically, Jesus Christ negated the Law and the Jews were offended by that. Jesus Christ presented a new way of grace that gives righteousness before God by faith alone. They could not understand this nor accept it. The whole idea of free mercy and grace through faith is a stone in their path which makes them stumble (v. 33).

Israel's Present
Romans 10:1-21

The subject of Romans 10 is given to us in the very first verse, "Brethren, my heart's desire and prayer to God for Israel is, that they might be saved." He had already said in Romans 9 that he could wish that he himself was accursed from Christ if it would bring the Jews to salvation. He had an intense burning desire for their salvation. The intent of Romans 10 is to show why the Jews have not found salvation and that they must be saved based on the same principles that save the gentiles. Paul's intense is an example for us. We also should desire Israel's salvation and pray for it.

The Jews have rejected the righteousness of God (Rom. 10:1-11).

1 ¶Brethren, my heart's desire and prayer to God for Israel is, that they might be saved.
2 For I bear them record that they have a zeal of God, but not according to knowledge.
3 For they being ignorant of God's righteousness, and going about to establish their own righteousness, have not submitted themselves unto the righteousness of God.
4 For Christ is the end of the law for righteousness to every one that believeth.
5 For Moses describeth the righteousness which is of the law, That the man which doeth those things shall live by them.
6 But the righteousness which is of faith speaketh on this wise, Say not in thine heart, Who shall ascend into heaven? (that is, to bring Christ down from above:)
7 Or, Who shall descend into the deep? (that is, to bring up Christ again from the dead.)
8 But what saith it? The word is nigh thee, even in thy mouth, and in thy heart: that is, the word of faith, which we preach;
9 That if thou shalt confess with thy mouth the Lord Jesus, and shalt believe in thine heart that God hath raised him from the dead, thou shalt be saved.
10 For with the heart man believeth unto righteousness; and with the mouth confession is made unto salvation.
11 For the scripture saith, Whosoever believeth on him shall not be ashamed.

The Jews rightly have zeal toward God, but their zeal operates in an atmosphere of ignorance. Religious zeal without knowledge of the truth leads to more errors than we realize. The seven major crusades from 1095 to 1291 AD were sanctioned by the Roman Catholic Church for the supposed goal of rescuing the Holy Land from the Muslims.[36] These actions were based on the erroneous belief that the Holy Land belongs to the Catholic Church. Religious motivations mixed with political motivations, without knowledge of the Scriptures on the matter, launched these military campaigns, death, and destruction. The Muslims did the same to conquer lands, spread their religion, and establish their caliphates. Cults and heresies of all kinds have been started by religious zeal without the knowledge of the truth. They all have the same result: the destruction of souls. Many of the participants end up deceived until it is too late and they spend eternity in Hell. This is why Paul was especially grieved for the Jews.

In the case of the Jews, their lack of knowledge led them to try to establish their own personal righteousness before God by keeping the Law of Moses (v. 3). Some form of salvation by good works is the major characteristic of all religions except *Biblical* Christianity. Buddhists have their list of standards to follow so they can improve their lot when they are reincarnated and eventually reach Nirvana (an extinction of personality and cessation of the reincarnation cycles). The Muslims have no assurance of salvation. It depends on how good a Muslim you were. The list goes on and on. The only faith that teaches that righteousness comes by God's grace through faith is *Biblical* Christianity. I emphasize the word "Biblical" because there are many faiths that are called "Christian," but they are not *Biblical*. Roman Catholicism is one of those, because it teaches salvation by a combination of faith and works.

The happy conclusion is that "Christ is the end of the law for righteousness to every one that believeth" (Rom. 10:4). We have already seen that the believer is no longer under the Law. Paul calls it "the ministration of condemnation" (2 Cor. 3: 9) and says that it "is abolished" (2 Cor. 3:13). We are justified; we are considered perfectly righteous in God's eyes. Since we know "that the law is not made for a righteous man, but for the lawless and disobedient, for the ungodly and for sinners" (1 Tim. 1:9), the Law no longer has *any authority* over a Christian. Righteousness comes from Jesus Christ by grace through faith. We no longer seek righteousness by keeping the law. Christ has ended that. However, the Jews do not understand these things. They think they are still under the Law and, perhaps, they still do not understand the demands of the Law. Verse five says the man who does them must live in them. Galatians states this very clearly, "For as many as are of the works of the law are under the curse: for it is written, Cursed is every one that continueth not in all things which are written in the book of the law to do them" (Gal. 3:10). All it takes is one violation to be guilty of all, to be a lawbreaker (James 2:10). Believers do not need to be concerned about the curse of the Law. A believer in Christ is never under a curse.

Verses six through eleven tells us what the righteousness which is of faith says. There is the negative, what it does not say (vv. 6-7), and there is the positive (vv. 8-11). Verses six through seven refer back to Deuteronomy

30:11-14, which says in part, "For this commandment which I command thee this day, it is not hidden from thee, neither is it far off. It is not in heaven, that thou shouldest say, Who shall go up for us to heaven, and bring it unto us, that we may hear it, and do it? Neither is it beyond the sea, that thou shouldest say, who shall go over the sea for us, and bring it unto us, that we may hear it, and do it" (Deut. 30:11-13)? If someone would bring word from Heaven that clearly would be the Lord Jesus, but it is not necessary because He has already given us the Word. In Romans 10:7, Paul took Moses' analogy of the sea a lot deeper until he reached Abraham's bosom (Luke 16:22), and said to bring the message from there would require that Christ be resurrected again. None of this is necessary because the Word is not far away; it is near to our hearts and mouths (v. 8; Deut, 30:14).

The heart and mouth are the key elements as to what brings salvation (vv. 9-11). This is a passage that is very familiar to Bible believers. This passage professes to tell us what brings salvation. The three required elements for salvation are: faith and confession with the mouth (v. 9), and prayer. Since the confession is from the mouth, then it is audible rather than just in the heart. However, faith, believing with your heart that God raised Christ from the dead, is the specific action that brings justification (vv. 10-11).

I would like to issue a challenge to my readers. It is abundantly clear throughout Romans up to this point and beyond (Rom. 11:6) that salvation is not by good works, but by faith. My challenge questions to you are these: Doesn't confession with the mouth and prayer, constitute some things I am *doing* to gain salvation? Doesn't prayer and confession with the mouth fall into the realm of *good works*? In Romans 10, Confession and prayer are given as conditions for salvation. On the other hand, Romans 10:14 clearly says that anyone who calls upon the name of the Lord has already believed and, therefore, is already justified (also see verse 10). Why is this introduced here, when it has not been mentioned at all in Romans 1:1-9:21? By the way, what about people who cannot speak? How are they to gain salvation?

The term "confession" is first mentioned in Romans 10 where it is mentioned twice. To confess the Lord Jesus is certainly something God expects of us as Christians, because He expects us to be witnesses (Acts 1:8). After Romans 10, confession and prayer are never again mentioned in the New Testament as a condition of salvation. 1 John 4:15 says that if you confess the Son, God dwells in you. However this is not saying that confession is a condition of salvation, but, rather, it is *evidence* that you are saved. In the Gospels and Acts, the word "confession" is not mentioned in reference to salvation unless it is Matthew 10:32 and Luke 12:8. These say that if you confess Christ before men, He will confess you before the angels, but if you do not confess Him before men He will not confess you in Heaven. These statements never say you will not be saved, if you fail to confess Him. It is explained in 2 Timothy 2:1; if we deny Him, He will deny us the right to reign with Him. Refusing to confess Christ before men is equal to denying Him. There are no other references to confession as a condition of salvation.

What about prayer? Many of us have been taught that when we are leading someone to Christ, we should lead them in "the sinner's prayer." Romans 10 makes prayer a condition of salvation; yet, as mentioned above, it is clear that only a believer can call upon the name of the Lord. "The" sinner's prayer is found nowhere in Scripture. Romans 10:14 emphasizes this by a question: "How then shall they call on him in whom they have not believed?" The closest thing to a prayer for salvation is found in Luke 18:10-14, where a publican (a Jew) is praying a prayer of repentance in the temple. I don't see any reason why we can't recommend this prayer when leading someone to Christ, but it's never said to be something a sinner *must* do to get saved.

    The phrase "call upon (or, on) the name of the Lord" is found eleven times in the Bible, eight times in the Old Testament and three times in the New Testament. Some of these are historical references to people calling on the Lord (Gen. 4:26; 1 Kings 18:24, 25; 2 Kings 5:11). One of those times in the Old Testament is Psalms 116:13, where the psalmist takes the cup of salvation *before* he calls on the name of the Lord. The other two are examples of Jews, *who are already saved,* calling on the Lord (Ps. 116:17; Zech. 3:9). One of the New Testament references is obviously in Romans 10. The other is 1 Corinthians 1:2 in which Paul addresses the letter "to them that are sanctified in Christ Jesus, called to be saints, with all that in every place call upon the name of Jesus Christ our Lord, both theirs and ours." This obviously refers to people who are already saved calling on the Lord. The third time is in Peter's sermon in Acts 2:21, where he quotes Joel 2:31 in a reference to the second coming. There is no enlightenment on the subject at hand from this verse in Acts, except that it is used in the same context as Romans 10 and it is addressed to Israel, not Gentiles. So, Romans 10 stands alone, but cannot be ignored because it is part of the inspired Word of God.

What does the total testimony of Scripture say about the conditions for salvation? To answer that question, I am not going to do anything except point to the references in the Bible, no logic and no philosophy. The chief reference is Eph. 2:8-9, "For by grace are ye saved through faith; and that not of yourselves: it is the gift of God: not of works, lest any man should boast." Even though this should be enough to tell us that getting saved involves *only* grace and faith, we will not leave it there. I will not quote John 3:16. You all should be familiar with that. It contains the words "whosoever believeth in him should not perish." John 3 does not stop at John 3:16. John 3:18 says, "He that believeth on him is not condemned." You will find the same in John 3:36; 5:24; Acts 8:37; 10:43; 13:39; 15:7, 11, 18; 16:31; 19:4; 20:21; 21:20; 26:20; Rom. 1:16; 4:5, 11, 24; 1 Cor. 1:21; 1 Cor. 15:1-4, 11; Gal. 3:6; Eph. 1:3, 19; 2 Thess. 2:13; 1 Thess. 4:14; 1 Tim. 1:16; etc. The only things mentioned in these and other verses are repentance and faith. Never is confession or prayer mentioned as a condition to get saved. Even the verses in Luke 18:10-14 does not recommend or command a sinner's prayer. It was not the prayer that justified the publican; it was faith (v. 14).

So, why is it mentioned in Romans 10? Confession and prayer are definitely presented there as conditions of salvation. There are only two possible answers to this that I am aware of. The first has to do with the Jews. Since Romans 10 (and Acts 2) is about the salvation of the Jews, then does God add conditions to the salvation of the Jews that are not required of Gentiles? In Acts 2, Peter is preaching Jesus to the assembled Jews on Pentecost. He seems to be recommending prayer for salvation. So is there an extra requirement for Jews? I reject that solution, because Romans 10:12 says that there is no difference between the Jew and the Gentile. Also, Acts 15:11, says, "But we believe that through the grace of the Lord Jesus Christ we shall be saved, even as they," indicating that the conditions of salvation are the same for both. Ephesians 2:8-9, salvation by grace through faith, applies to both Jews and Gentiles.

    The second solution requires that we cover some ground we have been over before. Salvation, the same as sanctification, comes in three tenses: past, present, and future. In this sense it is very close in meaning to sanctification. Sometimes the word "salvation" seems to be used as a general term to refer to all three tenses. In the past we were saved from the penalty of sin. In the present we are being saved from the power of sin in our daily lives and in the future we will be saved from the very presence of sin and from the wrath of God poured out on the world in the Tribulation period. Past salvation is mentioned in Acts 11:14; 16:30, 31; Rom. 1:16; 10:1; 11:14; 1 Cor. 1:18; 1:21; 15:2; 2 Cor. 2:15; Eph. 2:5, 8; 1 Thess. 2:16; 2 Thess. 2:10; 1 Tim. 2:4; and Titus 3:5. Present salvation is found in 2 Cor. 1:6; 7:8-10; Eph. 6:17; Phil. 1:19, 28; 2:12; 1 Tim. 4:16; and 2 Tim. 1:19. Future salvation is referred to in Rom. 5:9, 10; 8:24; 9:27; 11:26; 13:11; 1 Cor. 3:15; 5:5; and 1 Thess. 5:8, 9. Is it possible that the reference to salvation in Romans 10 is a reference to the present or future aspects of salvation? If so, that would make the statements of Romans 10 consistent with the teaching of salvation throughout the Pauline epistles.

Confession and calling on the Lord have some definite applications to present salvation and as a part of the sanctification process. The importance of prayer has already been seen in Romans 6 – 8. Luke 12:8 tells us that Jesus expects us to confess Him before men; declare before others that we know Him. One way of witnessing is to tell others how we came to know Him. The structure of a good personal witness of salvation is found in Acts 26, where Paul witnessed to King Agrippa. First, he told of his manner of life before he was saved (Acts 26:1-11), then he detailed how he got saved (Acts 26:12-18) and finally what happened after he got saved (Acts 26:19-22). At the end of his testimony, he gave the gospel (Acts 26:23-29).

Confession also helps keep our lives from sin. There must be a way to deal with the sin that occasionally happens. 1 John 1:8-9 says, "If we say that we have no sin, we deceive ourselves, and the truth is not in us. *If we confess our sins*, he is faithful and just to forgive us our sins, and to cleanse us from all unrighteousness." When we fail the Lord, and we certainly will, we need to take care of it in this manner right away. This is not an exhortation to confess to a priest. There are no priestly offices in the New Testament. This is an exhortation to take our sins directly to the Lord and confess them to Him. "Let us therefore come boldly unto the throne of grace, that we may obtain mercy, and find grace to help in time of need" (Heb. 4:16). There is no need for a human mediator on earth, "For there is one God, and one mediator between God and men, the man Christ Jesus" (1 Tim. 2:5).

Another application of the heart and the mouth to the sanctification aspect of salvation is found in Joshua 1:8, "This book of the law shall not depart out of thy mouth; but thou shalt meditate therein day and night, that thou mayest observe to do according to all that is written therein: for then thou shalt make thy way prosperous, and then thou shalt have good success." This command is to meditate in the Word of God and its application goes beyond just the Law (which included the first five books of the Bible). At that time, the only thing they had was the Law. Meditation is clearly a thinking process that takes place in the mind and heart. Yet, the verse says, "shall not depart out of thy mouth." Does that mean we should think out loud? Not at all. Jesus told us that "out of the abundance of the heart the mouth speaketh" (Mt. 12:34). What you fill your heart with will definitely come out of your mouth. So, fill your heart with the Word of God. "Let the word of Christ dwell in you richly in all wisdom" (Col. 3:16). You will not be able to keep your mouth from confessing Christ. Your relationship to Him will be confirmed to the public by your speech.

The Gospel Applied to the Jews
(Rom. 10:12-21)

12 ¶For there is no difference between the Jew and the Greek: for the same Lord over all is rich unto all that call upon him.
13 For whosoever shall call upon the name of the Lord shall be saved.
14 How then shall they call on him in whom they have not believed? and how shall they believe in him of whom they

have not heard? and how shall they hear without a preacher?
15 And how shall they preach, except they be sent? as it is written, How beautiful are the feet of them that preach the gospel of peace, and bring glad tidings of good things!
16 But they have not all obeyed the gospel. For Esaias saith, Lord, who hath believed our report?
17 So then faith cometh by hearing, and hearing by the word of God.
18 But I say, Have they not heard? Yes verily, their sound went into all the earth, and their words unto the ends of the world.
19 But I say, Did not Israel know? First Moses saith, I will provoke you to jealousy by them that are no people, and by a foolish nation I will anger you.
20 But Esaias is very bold, and saith, I was found of them that sought me not; I was made manifest unto them that asked not after me.
21 But to Israel he saith, All day long I have stretched forth my hands unto a disobedient and gainsaying people.

Romans 10:12-21 applies the gospel to the Jews. It is clear that "there is no difference" (v. 12). Everyone must go through the same process that is outlined in verses twelve to fifteen. That process is 1) God sends a preacher, 2) the preacher preaches the gospel, 3) the sinner hears the gospel, 4) the sinner believes the gospel, and 5) the believer calls upon the name of the Lord. It is clear that the prayer comes after faith; "How then shall they call on him in whom they have not believed?" It is faith alone that justifies. "For with the heart man believeth unto righteousness" (v. 10)

This also tells us that the preaching of the gospel is central. It is the key to winning people to Christ. The human heart is naturally resistant to the gospel. Some cultures are worse in this than others, but the root cause is the same. Jesus said, "And this is the condemnation, that light is come into the world, and men loved darkness rather than light, because their deeds were evil. For every one that doeth evil hateth the light, neither cometh to the light, lest his deeds should be reproved" (John 3:19-20). Some come up with all kinds of plans to attract people and soften their hearts toward Christ and the gospel. God may use some of this, but the Holy Spirit has not come to soothe or coax the flesh. He has come to *reprove the world*. "And when he is come, he will reprove the world of sin, and of righteousness, and of judgment" (John 16:8). The Holy Spirit's purpose is to confront the love of darkness in men's hearts and bring them face to face with a Holy God. He is *not* interested in convincing the world that *Judeo-Christian values* are best. He wants to strip men and women of their excuses and boldly confront them with *God's truth*. This world will never be won by Judeo-Christian values, but *only by the gospel of Jesus Christ*.

It is true that the rebellious heart of human beings will never turn to God on its own. People need the intervention of God. "No man can come to me, except the Father which hath sent me draw him" (John 6:44). The Father must be at work in a sinner's heart to draw him to Christ. But, how does that happen? Jesus went on to tell us. "It is written in the prophets, and they shall be all taught of God. Every man therefore that hath heard, and hath learned of the Father, cometh unto me" (John 6:45). Everyone who hears and learns comes to Christ. Many refuse to hear and some who hear refuse to learn. How do they hear? What does Romans 10:17 say? "So then faith cometh by hearing, and hearing by the word of God." Hearing comes by the Word of God, so the drawing power of God works through the preaching of the gospel. Jesus assured us that He would draw all to Himself. "And I, if I be lifted up from the earth, will draw all men unto me" (John 12:32).

Not everyone has obeyed the gospel (v. 16). To obey the gospel is to believe. In Romans 10:18-19, God asks two questions. The first is, "Have they not heard?" The obvious answer to this question is, yes, they have heard. Then, He refers to Ps. 19:1-6.

> *The heavens declare the glory of God; and the firmament sheweth his handiwork. Day unto day uttereth speech, and night unto night sheweth knowledge. There is no speech nor language, where their voice is not heard. Their line is gone out through all the earth, and their words to the end of the world. In them hath he set a tabernacle for the sun, which is as a bridegroom coming out of his chamber, and rejoiceth as a strong man to run a race. His going forth is from the end of the heaven, and his circuit unto the ends of it: and there is nothing hid from the heat thereof.*

"The heavens declare the glory of God ... There is no speech nor language, where their voice is not heard." There are many references to the "general" revelation of God in nature, such as, Romans 1:18-20, which says that we can know the power and greatness of God through nature. However, Romans 10 seems to say that sinners can learn something of the gospel from the heavens. Genesis 1:14 says that the sun, moon, and stars are not just for days and years and seasons, but also for *signs*. This revelation is enough to make men without excuse before God. However, God does not depend on creation or the stars to evangelize the world. That job is given to believers, who are commanded to preach the gospel to every creature in every nation (Mt. 28:19-20; Mark 16:15).

The second question (v. 19) is "Did not Israel know?" The obvious answer to this question is the same answer as the first, yes. The first of two answers reveals one of the reasons God opened the door of the gospel to the Gentiles. He wished to provoke Israel to jealousy. This is affirmed in verse 20. He wanted to move the Jews to desire the blessings that the Gentiles were receiving. The final statement (v. 21) shows that they refused to listen regardless of what motivation God gave them.

The Future of Israel
Romans 11:1-36

The gospel has been extended to the Gentiles and many of them have come to Christ, but most have not. The Jews rejected Jesus Christ when He claimed to be their Messiah (John 1:11-13). They are now in a general state of blindness. So, what is to be their fate as a nation? Has God cast them off and given their promises to the Gentile church? No, not at all! "Hath God cast away his people?

God forbid ... God hath not cast away his people which he foreknew" (Rom. 11:1-2). Romans 11 confirms God's promises to Israel and He confirms the glorious future of the nation.

God's current view of Israel's salvation
(Rom. 11:1-6)

1 I say then, Hath God cast away his people? God forbid. For I also am an Israelite, of the seed of Abraham, of the tribe of Benjamin.
2 God hath not cast away his people which he foreknew. Wot ye not what the scripture saith of Elias? how he maketh intercession to God against Israel, saying,
3 Lord, they have killed thy prophets, and digged down thine altars; and I am left alone, and they seek my life.
4 But what saith the answer of God unto him? I have reserved to myself seven thousand men, who have not bowed the knee to the image of Baal.
5 Even so then at this present time also there is a remnant according to the election of grace.
6 And if by grace, then is it no more of works: otherwise grace is no more grace. But if it be of works, then is it no more grace: otherwise work is no more work.

Since Jews are under condemnation the same as the Gentiles and they must come to Christ in the same way Gentiles must. Only those who believe will be saved. However, the reference to God comforting Elijah (Elias in Greek) by the fact that there were 7000 Israelites who had not bowed the knee to the false god Baal (1 Kings 19:9-18), shows that God always has at least a small number, a remnant, who believe. Not everyone refuses the truth. Paul uses himself as an example and includes himself in that remnant. This remnant which has believed is called the "election of grace," the chosen ones of God's grace. What a blessing it is to be one of those! Then Paul ends the paragraph with a very strong emphasis on the fact that this grace that has made us elect totally rules out works. Works and grace are mutually exclusive. Most of Israel seeks righteousness by good works, which would make any righteousness achieved nothing but self-righteousness. Isaiah said, "But we are all as an unclean thing, and all our righteousnesses (righteous works) are as filthy rags" (Is. 64:6). Their approach cuts them off from God's grace.

The Blindness of Israel
And Enlightenment of the Gentiles
(Rom. 11:7-24)

7 What then? Israel hath not obtained that which he seeketh for; but the election hath obtained it, and the rest were blinded
8 (According as it is written, God hath given them the spirit of slumber, eyes that they should not see, and ears that they should not hear;) unto this day.
9 And David saith, Let their table be made a snare, and a trap, and a stumblingblock, and a recompence unto them:
10 Let their eyes be darkened, that they may not see, and bow down their back alway.
11 I say then, Have they stumbled that they should fall? God forbid: but rather through their fall salvation is come unto

the Gentiles, for to provoke them to jealousy.
12 Now if the fall of them be the riches of the world, and the diminishing of them the riches of the Gentiles; how much more their fulness?
13 For I speak to you Gentiles, inasmuch as I am the apostle of the Gentiles, I magnify mine office:
14 If by any means I may provoke to emulation them which are my flesh, and might save some of them.
15 For if the casting away of them be the reconciling of the world, what shall the receiving of them be, but life from the dead?

The elect (those who believed) have found righteousness (justification), but the rest *were blinded* (vv. 7-10). This blindness is also called "the spirit of slumber," "eyes that cannot see," "ears that cannot hear," (v. 8) and "darkened eyes" (v. 10). Paul refers back to Isaiah 29:10 in verse eight and Psalms 69:22-24 in verse nine. Jesus spoke of this also when He explained the use of parables to His Apostles.

> *Therefore speak I to them in parables: because they seeing see not; and hearing they hear not, neither do they understand. And in them is fulfilled the prophecy of Esaias, which saith, By hearing ye shall hear, and shall not understand; and seeing ye shall see, and shall not perceive: For this people's heart is waxed gross, and their ears are dull of hearing, and their eyes they have closed; lest at any time they should see with their eyes, and hear with their ears, and*

should understand with their heart, and should be converted, and I should heal them. (Mt. 13:13-15)

So, God blinded the minds of the Jews who did not believe. However, this was no spiteful reaction or arbitrary decision. This was God's judgment after they had already refused to hear and believe. Paul says it is a "recompense," a pay back (Rom. 10:9). Jesus said their hearts were "waxed gross, and their ears are dull of hearing, their eyes *they have closed.*" The blindness God gave them was recompense for the fact that they had *already willfully closed their own eyes and ears.* "He came unto his own, and his own received him not" (John 1:11). Rejection of the truth is a dangerous thing. Take heed, "if ye seek him, he will be found of you; but if ye forsake him, he will forsake you" (2 Chron. 15:2). "Today if ye will hear his voice, Harden not your hearts"(Heb. 3:7-8).

Israel has temporarily fallen from its lofty place of favor as God's people (Romans 11:11-15). The immediate result of this was to open the door of the gospel to the Gentiles. The diminishing of the Jews has greatly enriched the Gentiles. When Israel is restored the riches will be much greater. Paul says it will be life from the dead. Indeed, this is true. Israel will be finally restored to favor and greatness when Jesus returns to rule in the Millennial Kingdom. That will be the time when the first resurrection of the righteous is complete (Rev. 20:1-6). The saved Jews at Christ's coming and all the righteous resurrected Jewish and Gentile dead will enter the kingdom together.

The Two Olive Trees
(Rom. 11:16-24)

A picture of two olive trees is used in Romans 11:16-24 to illustrate this cutting off and restoration of Israel along with the offer of the gospel to the Gentiles.

16 For if the firstfruit be holy, the lump is also holy: and if the root be holy, so are the branches.
17 And if some of the branches be broken off, and thou, being a wild olive tree, wert graffed in among them, and with them partakest of the root and fatness of the olive tree;
18 Boast not against the branches. But if thou boast, thou bearest not the root, but the root thee.
19 Thou wilt say then, The branches were broken off, that I might be graffed in.
20 Well; because of unbelief they were broken off, and thou standest by faith. Be not highminded, but fear:
21 For if God spared not the natural branches, take heed lest he also spare not thee.
22 Behold therefore the goodness and severity of God: on them which fell, severity; but toward thee, goodness, if thou continue in his goodness: otherwise thou also shalt be cut off.
23 And they also, if they abide not still in unbelief, shall be graffed in: for God is able to graff them in again.
24 For if thou wert cut out of the olive tree which is wild by nature, and wert graffed contrary to nature into a good olive tree: how much more shall these, which be the naturalbranches, be graffed into their own olive tree?

One Olive tree is the natural domestic tree, grown and cultivated by the farmer. The other is a wild olive tree that has grown by itself in the brush away from the farm. The first represents Israel and the second represents the Gentiles. This clearly shows that the domestic natural olive tree has not been cut down and cast aside. The wild tree has not been substituted for the natural tree. The natural olive tree is still the main tree. What has happened is that some of the natural branches have been broken off and wild branches from the wild tree have been grafted in. The natural tree is still the one from which the blessings of God flow, but now many of the wild branches broken from the wild tree and grafted onto the natural tree are receiving the many of the blessings of the natural tree. They did not have to become Jews to get these blessings. They simply had to believe the gospel. The natural branches that were cut off were lost because they refused to believe the gospel. God could easily reverse the situation, so Gentiles had better take advantage of the opportunity and turn to God while they can.

In the End, All Israel will be Saved
(Rom. 11:25-32)

25 For I would not, brethren, that ye should be ignorant of this mystery, lest ye should be wise in your own conceits; that blindness in part is happened to Israel, until the fulness of the Gentiles be come in.
26 And so all Israel shall be saved: as it is written, There shall come out of Sion the Deliverer, and shall turn away ungodliness from Jacob:

27 For this is my covenant unto them, when I shall take away their sins.
28 As concerning the gospel, they are enemies for your sakes: but as touching the election, they are beloved for the fathers' sakes.
29 For the gifts and calling of God are without repentance.
30 For as ye in times past have not believed God, yet have now obtained mercy through their unbelief:
31 Even so have these also now not believed, that through your mercy they also may obtain mercy.
32 For God hath concluded them all in unbelief, that he might have mercy upon all.

Finally, there is a time limit on the partial blindness of Israel and on the opportunity of the Gentiles. The time continues until "the fullness of the Gentiles" has come in. At the end "all Israel shall be saved." The restoration of Israel is foretold in places like Jeremiah 30:10-11; 16:14-15; 24:6; Amos 9:14-15; Ezek. 37:12-14. The quote in Romans 11:26-27 is not found in the Old Testament precisely in this form. It is a teaching that is taken from more than one place in the Old Testament. Suggestions are Ps. 14:7; Is. 59:20; with Is. 27:9. [37]

The "fullness of the Gentiles" would be the maximum number of the Gentiles who will be saved. God knows what that number is and when it will occur. One thing that is certain is that the fullness of the Gentiles will not occur in the church dispensation. Before the Tribulation starts on earth the church will be called out of the world and gathered together in the air, where we will meet the Lord (1 Thess. 4:13-18). During the time of Tribulation, following the departure of the church from the world, God will pour out His wrath on a sinful world. At that time, there will be such a great number of Gentiles saved that they cannot be numbered (Rev. 7:9-17). These will be the final Gentiles saved from the penalty of sin; the fullness of the Gentiles will have come in. After that all Israel will be saved. This doesn't mean that every individual Jew who ever lived will be saved. Rather, all the members of the nation who believe will enter the Millennial Kingdom, know the Lord, and have His Spirit (Jer. 31:33-34; Rom. 11:27).

      The Jews presently are considered enemies of the gospel (v. 28). In many examples given in the Book of Acts and in Paul's letters, they opposed the gospel to the point of violence. For example, Paul encountered Jews in Acts 13 who raised trouble because the Gentiles were listening to him. Paul and Barnabas moved on to Lystra, but the Jews of Antioch and Iconium followed him, drew him out of the city, and stoned him (Acts 14:19). Although Israel is the enemy of the gospel now, all Israel is beloved for the sake of the fathers, Abraham, Isaac, and Jacob. The fact that God loves them will not change because of the principle of Romans 11:29, "For the gifts and calling of God are without repentance." This statement is meant as a guarantee that all God gave Israel is certain and all His Promises to them will be fulfilled.

      When God gives gifts and God gives a calling, He does not change His mind. This is a principal that applies to many things. It is a promise from God. Bear this in mind when considering the gifts and calling God has given you. It means that once God has called and once he has given a gift, He does not change his mind. Are you saved? He has called you by the gospel and He is not sorry. He has given you the gift of eternal life and He will not take it away. He gave it to you by grace and He lets you keep it by grace. Has God gifted you with a spiritual ability for His service (1 Cor. 12)? He will not remove it from you. Don't let it be wasted.

The calling of God is an interesting subject. We are all called to a "vocation" (Eph. 4:1-3), which involves holiness of life and love for the brethren. Regarding a call to service, Paul said he was called to be an apostle (Rom. 1:1), but he was not called to a specific location of service. Sometimes we think that God has called us to Germany or Togo or South Africa. That is not necessarily so. Paul was called to be an apostle wherever he was. He was in Ephesus now and Corinth then, but wherever he was he was an apostle. I have a friend who has been called to be a pastor-teacher. He has used this calling and gift in Romania and now he is a pastor in the USA. Another friend had a similar calling and served in Central America, the Philippines, Hungary, and the USA. Similarly, a Christian who is gifted with the gift of showing mercy can fulfill that gift in any church he attends. The place of service may change, but the calling and gifts do not.

Romans 11:30-32 concludes the matter. We were unbelievers and now because God has turned from the Jews, who refused to believe the gospel and receive their Messiah, we have been given mercy. At the same time, the means by which we have received mercy, the grace of our God through His Son, Jesus Christ, has also become the means by which the Jews can receive mercy. The way of salvation offered by the Lord Jesus Christ is free to Jew and Gentile alike.

The chapter concludes with a burst of praise. God is the only one who is worthy of glory and praise.

> 33 ¶O the depth of the riches both of the wisdom and knowledge of God! how unsearchable are his judgments, and his ways past finding out!
> 34 For who hath known the mind of the Lord? or who hath been his counsellor?
> 35 Or who hath first given to him, and it shall be recompensed unto him again?
> 36 For of him, and through him, and to him, are all things: to whom be glory for ever. Amen.

How beautifully God has worked all this out! This is an exaltation of His wisdom and knowledge. All that God does is a result of His wisdom and knowledge. It is so deep that we will never understand it all in this life.

> The rest of the chapter is an outburst of wonder and praise. From a mountain height the apostle surveys the sublime plan of God, and his soul breaks out in a transport of delight. In this wonderful plan for the salvation of Jew and Gentile there is an unfathomable depth of riches, and wisdom, and knowledge." [38]

Chapter Six

The Dedication of the Believer's Life
Romans 12:1-15:13

A comment in *Halley's Bible Handbook* is particularly appropriate for this last major section of the Book of Romans.

> Paul invariable closed any theological discussion with an earnest exhortation to a Christian Manner of Life. And so it is here. In previous chapters he has been insisting that our standing before God depends wholly on the Mercy of Christ, and not on our own Good Works. Here he is equally insistent that that Mercy, which so graciously forgives, is the very thing that supplies us with a powerful and irresistible Urge to Good Works, and Transforms our whole outlook on life. [39]

These chapters take the matter of sanctification of the Christian and move it to the next step: the utter and complete dedication of the believer's life to Christ and the resulting changes in attitudes and behaviors. Charles Ryrie, in *Balancing the Christian Life*, says this about dedication:

> There is perhaps no more important matter in relation to the spiritual life than dedication. And yet this very basic concept is often confused especially when it is made a part of "formulas" for victorious living. Some present dedication as the entire answer to all the problems of the Christian life; others give it little place; and most do not understand the place of rededication in the whole matter. To be confused at this point is to do damage to the entire biblical teaching on Christian living. [40]

Dedication and Transformation of the Believer
Romans 12:1-2

1 I beseech you therefore, brethren, by the mercies of God, that ye present your bodies a living sacrifice, holy, acceptable unto God, which is your reasonable service.
2 And be not conformed to this world: but be ye transformed by the renewing of your mind, that ye may prove what is that good, and acceptable, and perfect, will of God.

The basis of dedication is the mercies of God. "I beseech you therefore, brethren, by the mercies of God …"

Dedication is based on the things God has done for us. In Romans 12:1, the foundation for a total giving of one's self and life to Christ is all the mercy described in the previous eleven chapters. God has taken us disobedient God-hating sinners and given us mercy, forgiveness, justification, reconciliation, transformation, new life, freedom from the domination of sin, the indwelling Spirit of God, eternal security, and the promise of glorification. This was all done because of the blood Christ shed on the cross to purchase us (1 Cor. 6:19-20) and give us redemption (Rom. 3:24). We owe our lives and our eternity to God's grace through Jesus Christ. "We love him, because he first loved us" (1 John 4:19). If we love Him, we will keep His commandments (John 14:21).

What is to be dedicated? The answer is to "present your bodies a living sacrifice, holy, acceptable unto God, which is your reasonable service" (Rom. 12:1). We present our bodies to God completely. The Old Testament illustration of this is the *burnt offering* (e.g. Ex. 29:18). When the animal is put on the altar for a burnt offering, it is *completely consumed*. We can assume that when the body is presented it carries the whole person with it. So, the dedication of Romans 12:1 is a *total dedication of oneself to God*.

Dedication is not a process. It is a decision a believer makes at some point in time. Dr. Ryrie explains it this way:

> This is represented in the Greek by the aorist infinitive used here ... Now the aorist represents an action as a point or an event even though it may cover a short or long period of time. But it

does not present the action as a series of repeated acts as does the present tense, for example. [41]

Earlier we saw the command to "yield yourselves unto God" (Rom. 6:13). "Submit yourselves therefore to God" (James 4:7). "For ye are bought with a price: therefore glorify God in your body, and in your spirit, which are God's" (1 Cor. 6:20). These are actions we are commanded to do in each battle with temptation, but this dedication is a one-time dedication that determines the course of our lives. It is a decision you make that your life will be lived to glorify and obey God. It will not only belong to God, but it will be lived for Him and Him alone. The total dedication of the believer's life to the will of God is a single event that affects all the rest of life. It is a *decision, attitude, and commitment of the heart.* This is a necessary event that sets the course of life for a believer. It makes the difference as to whether that life will work toward its potential in Christ and glorify God or be characterized by mediocrity. I am convinced there are many Christians who have never come to this point of dedication.

Dedication is also presented as "acceptable to God" and it is also considered to be "reasonable." This makes sense in the light of all that God has done for us. In view of the fact that the Lord Jesus gave His body and His life for us, it is certainly reasonable that you should give your body and life for Christ.

We are not to be conformed to the world. "And be not conformed to this world" (Romans 12:2). The dedication event of verse one is to result in non-conformity to the world. This is a command and it is *not* a single event. Rather, it is a day-by-day effort to not allow yourself to be like the world. We are not to act like the world when it would be contrary to God's Biblical standards nor are we to think like the world when it is contrary to the Scriptures. We are to live God's standards in the world and we are to carry God's thoughts into the world and express them in our behavior and speech. This will cause some to "think it strange that ye run not with them to the same excess of riot, speaking evil of you" (1 Peter 4:4). Yet, it is God's will to "purify unto himself a peculiar people, zealous of good works" (Titus 2:14).

> TRUTH: There is a powerful pull to be conformed to this world!
>
> Every day you are bombarded with anti-God thoughts from the T.V., Radio, Newspapers, advertisements, friends and marxist education.
>
> The media outlets have been sexualized, radicalized, demonized, socialized, and revolutionize.
>
> Institutes of Education have become radical platforms to introduce socialism and Marxism.
>
> Churches are no longer "Onward Christian Soldiers", but tamed tolerant kittens that bow and conform to this world.
>
> Preachers, stop conforming and start transforming!

> Christians, stop conforming and start transforming!
>
> Our churches sound like a local rock concert and Christians sound like the average lost person on the street.
>
> You are to be separated and sanctified. If you are not sanctified then you are not separated from this world, but part of it.
>
> God cannot show his power when you are part of the problem.
>
> You can know what is good, and acceptable and perfect, but to do that you have to know what is the "will of God" and His WILL is never to be conformed but to be transformed. [42]

Non-conformity to the world does not mean that we have to dress and act in a way that is totally out of step with the general culture around us, in the same manner as the Amish or German Baptists. It means that we are to find and do the will of God in our culture. That will is found in the Bible. Some of what we do may be out of step with the culture when the culture is out of step with God. An example of this is the command for women to dress modestly (1 Timothy 2:9). A godly woman will follow this command. Many unsaved women may do otherwise, while calling godly women "prudes."

We are to be transformed; "be ye transformed by the renewing of your mind" (Rom. 12:2). Once again this also is a process that will take time, but it is set in motion by the single event of dedication. The Greek word for *transformed* is the word from which we get our word *metamorphosis*. It is translated in the KJV as transformed, changed (2 Cor. 3:18), and transfigured (Mark 9:2). So, it is used for the transfiguration of Christ and of our own transfiguration into the image of Christ in 2 Corinthians 3:18: "But we all, with open face beholding as in a glass the glory of the Lord, are changed into the same image from glory to glory, even as by the Spirit of the Lord." We are new creatures when we begin the Christian life (2 Cor. 5:17) and we are changed to be like Christ from day to day after that. This is what Christian growth is all about (1 Peter 2:2; 2 Peter 3:18).

The means by which we are transformed is "the renewing of your mind" (Rom. 12:2). How is your mind renewed? 2 Corinthians 3:18 gives us the clue. It says that we behold the glory of the Lord in a glass (mirror). In James 1:22-24, the glass is the Word of God. So, it is the Word of God that changes (transforms) us to the image of the glory of the Lord. Therefore, it is the Word that renews our minds. Notice that the two references about growth above speak of knowledge and the Word. It is the word of God that gives us the mind of Christ; "Let this mind be in you, which was also in Christ Jesus" (Phil 2:5). The Word of God changes our way of thinking, our attitudes, our beliefs, our hopes, our dreams, our desires, and even our feelings. If the dedication of verse one is in place, it will change our way of living and behaving. We must saturate our minds with the Word of God. This requires far more than going to church and hearing the Word preached. You need to also put plans in place to read, study, memorize, and meditate on the Word of God.

The purpose of our transformation and renewing of mind is "that ye may prove what is that good, and acceptable, and perfect, will of God" (v.2). The word "prove" means to put to the test. Is God's will reallly good, acceptable, and perfect? That premise is put to the test in our lives and practice. We prove God's will is best by putting it into practice. To whom do we prove this? Other Christians and the world are convinced that God's will is good and right when they see it in practice. "Let your light so shine before men, that they may see your good works, and glorify your Father which is in heaven" (Mt. 5:16).

The Bible does not speak of a "rededication." The picture of the Christian life given in the Scriptures is one in which the initial dedication never needs to be redone. If a Christian sins, the dedication has been violated. What is needed then is immediate confession of sin to God (1 John 1:9). However, if a Christian has so gotten off the track of right living that he feels a new dedication should be made, then by all means do it, but do not forget the necessity to confess to God as needed.

Gifts in the Church
(Romans 12:3-8)

3 For I say, through the grace given unto me, to every man that is among you, not to think of himself more highly than he ought to think; but to think soberly, according as God hath dealt to every man the measure of faith.
4 For as we have many members in one body, and all members have not the same office:
5 So we, being many, are one body in Christ, and every one

members one of another.
6 Having then gifts differing according to the grace that is given to us, whether prophecy, let us prophesy according to the proportion of faith;
7 Or ministry, let us wait on our ministering: or he that teacheth, on teaching;
8 Or he that exhorteth, on exhortation: he that giveth, let him do it with simplicity; he that ruleth, with diligence; he that sheweth mercy, with cheerfulness.

What follows is a series of specific standards of conduct and attitude in the will of God, starting with spiritual gifts. It begins with the exhortation that you not think of yourself more highly than is realistic. There is no sin in accepting reality. Are you a talented person? Then it is alright to recognize that fact, but also recognize it is God who gave you the talents. You also need to recognize that being talented does not make you superior to others. They have talents, too. If you think you are more than you are or your talents make you better than others, it is pride and sin.

> *6 And these things, brethren, I have in a figure transferred to myself and to Apollos for your sakes; that ye might learn in us not to think of men above that which is written, that no one of you be puffed up for one against another.*
> *7 For who maketh thee to differ from another? and what hast thou that thou didst not receive? now if thou didst receive it, why dost thou glory, as if thou hadst not received it?* (1 Cor. 4:6-7).

All of the exhortations in chapter 12 should be viewed in the context of the church. 1 Corinthians 12 expands on the explanation of gifts given in verses 4 and 5. The church is the body of Christ (1 Cor. 12:13; Eph. 1:22-23). Just as each of us has one body and many parts or members, so is the body of Christ (1 Cor. 12:12). We are each a part or member of a much larger community. It is within that community that we exercise our gifts. Every member is necessary. None can be left out (1 Cor. 12:14-22). Even those members who have a gift that seems small and inconsequential are necessary (1 Cor. 12:23-27).

Paul outlines the place of spiritually gifted individuals in the church. These gifts are given by the spirit of God and are for the purpose of building up the church members. Everyone gets a gift, which is defined a special ability to serve other Christians (1 Cor. 12:7). According to 1 Corinthians 12:4-6, the gifts fall into two categories: administrations and operations. Administration includes apostles, pastors, rulers, governments, and certain kinds of helps (1 Cor. 12:28; Rom. 12:6-8; Eph. 4). Operation includes apostles, prophets, pastors, teachers, ministry, exhortation, showing mercy, giving, miracles, healing, and tongues. Miracles, healing, and tongues were sign gifts given to confirm the preached Word (Mark 16:20). They were primarily directed toward Jews (1 Cor. 1:22; 14:22). Historically, in the Book of Acts and beyond, as the New Testament was more and more written, these sign gifts gradually faded off the scene. That is not to say that God does not still perform miracles. Rather, it is to say that God no longer gifts men to be miracle workers.

Relationships in the Church and Other Exhortations
(Rom. 12:9-21)

9 Let love be without dissimulation. Abhor that which is evil; cleave to that which is good.
10 Be kindly affectioned one to another with brotherly love; in honour preferring one another;
11 Not slothful in business; fervent in spirit; serving the Lord;
12 Rejoicing in hope; patient in tribulation; continuing instant in prayer;
13 Distributing to the necessity of saints; given to hospitality.
14 Bless them which persecute you: bless, and curse not.
15 Rejoice with them that do rejoice, and weep with them that weep.
16 Be of the same mind one toward another. Mind not high things, but condescend to men of low estate. Be not wise in your own conceits.
17 Recompense to no man evil for evil. Provide things honest in the sight of all men.
18 If it be possible, as much as lieth in you, live peaceably with all men.
19 Dearly beloved, avenge not yourselves, but rather give place unto wrath: for it is written, Vengeance is mine; I will repay, saith the Lord.
20 Therefore if thine enemy hunger, feed him; if he thirst, give him drink: for in so doing thou shalt heap coals of fire on his head.
21 Be not overcome of evil, but overcome evil with good.

Loving Relationships Between Christians

The majority of the standards listed in this section are about relationships. The two major things covered in this chapter that make for peace in the church are wise use of spiritual gifts and love. The overall standard for the Christian life is to "Let love be without dissimulation. Abhor that which is evil; cleave to that which is good" (v. 9).

"Let love be without dissimulation" (v. 9). The word "dissimulation" means hypocritical, not real, pretended. "Hereby perceive we the love of God, because he laid down his life for us: and we ought to lay down our lives for the brethren. But whoso hath this world's good, and seeth his brother have need, and shutteth up his bowels of compassion from him, how dwelleth the love of God in him? My little children, let us not love in word, neither in tongue; but in deed and in truth" (1 John 3:16-18; see John 15:12; Phil. 1:9).

The exhortation to love in reality and not pretense is followed in verse ten with "Be kindly affectioned one to another with brotherly love." Love between Christians is to be more than dry sterile duty and action. There is to be an attitude and feeling with it. The feeling is "affection." There is also to a "tenderhearted" attitude.

I didn't fully understand this until recent years. My ministry takes me to various parts of the world. When I visited the brethren engaged in Bible translation in China the first time, found myself falling in love with the believers there and the Chinese people in general. We held a translation conference for Christian leaders in Techiman, Ghana, West Africa. The conference was a little piece of heaven and my heart was full of affection for my fellow Christians there. When I went to Togo, West Africa to hold a translation conference there, I fell in love again. Where ever I go I seem to experience this to one degree or another. There is a deep unbreakable heart connection between believers.

"*Abhor that which is evil; cleave to that which is good*" (v. 9). "Abhor means to "hate extremely, or with contempt; to loathe, detest." [43] As in love, there is a feeling and attitude toward evil also. It is to have a negative effect on our emotions. The Greek word for "cleave" means "to glue together." [44] Your heart is to be tied inseparably to that which is good. The particular evil in view here is probably evil in relationships, such as, hatred, malice, and unkindness, because it is sandwiched between a call to let love be real (v. 9) and an exhortation to kind affection (v. 10).

"*In honour preferring one another*"(v. 10): "Honor" is the "esteem due or paid to worth; high estimation." [45] To the esteem we may add respect. The Scripture says, "Let nothing be done through strife or vainglory; but in lowliness of mind let each esteem other better than themselves. Look not every man on his own things, but every man also on the things of others" (Phil. 3-4). Love prefers to lift up others rather than oneself, because love "seeketh not her own" (1 Cor. 13:5).

Love is seen in "*distributing to the necessity of saints; given to hospitality*" (v. 13). Once again the importance of love being practical action is reinforced. Kind affection toward once another must result in care for one another. If we love the brethren we will want to associate with them in church and in our homes and care for their needs.

"*Rejoice with them that do rejoice, and weep with them that weep*" (v. 15). To rejoice with someone means to be glad or happy. [46] When someone is experiencing a happy situation or going through a sad and difficult problem, we need to offer more than an understanding ear. Listening sympathetically can be a great help and encouragement to others, but to be empathetic, to feel with them, is even more helpful.

"*Be of the same mind one toward another*" (v. 16). "Same mind" speaks of an important concept frequently repeated in the New Testament. A similar term is *likeminded*. "Only let your conversation be as it becometh the gospel of Christ: that whether I come and see you, or else be absent, I may hear of your affairs, that ye stand fast in *one spirit*, with *one mind* striving together for the faith of the gospel" (Phil. 1:27). *One mind* and *one spirit* speaks is more than simply agreement. It describes unity among believers. That unity is centered around an attitude of acceptance and love toward one another. Humility, compassion, understanding, and provision are words that describe it.

> 2 Fulfil ye my joy, that ye be likeminded, having the same love, being of one accord, of one mind.
> 3 Let nothing be done through strife or vainglory; but in lowliness of mind let each esteem other better than themselves.
> 4 Look not every man on his own things, but every man also on the things of others.
> 5 Let this mind be in you, which was also in Christ Jesus" (Phil. 2:2-4).

Being of one mind does not mean that we are to be in complete agreement on *everything*. Philippians 2:2-5 above describes some of the content of this unity. We are to be likeminded in love. We are to have the same love for all. Further, we are to seek the good, welfare, and exaltation of others more than ourselves. We are to hold others high in our esteem. We are to exhibit humility of mind toward others. This is the mind of Jesus Christ, who left His glory and made Himself a servant. So, to be likeminded is to have the mind of Jesus Christ. Once again the Scriptures are the only place we can learn what that mind is.

"*Mind not high things, but condescend to men of low estate*" (V. 16). In the vernacular that is *get off your high horse!* The word for mind is also used in Romans 12:2-3 in regard to *thinking* of oneself higher than we should. To *mind* something means to be mentally disposed toward it or to be intensely interested in it. "High things" are associated with pride or things held in high esteem among men (Job 41:34; Prov. 21:4; Luke 16:15). In this context of relationships and love, the applicable example is that of showing respect of persons in the Book of James.

> *1 My brethren, have not the faith of our Lord Jesus Christ, the Lord of glory, with respect of persons.*
> *2 For if there come unto your assembly a man with a gold ring, in goodly apparel, and there come in also a poor man in vile raiment;*
> *3 And ye have respect to him that weareth the gay clothing, and say unto him, Sit thou here in a good place; and say to the poor, Stand thou there,*

> *or sit here under my footstool:*
> *4 Are ye not then partial in yourselves, and are become judges of evil thoughts?*
> *5 Hearken, my beloved brethren, Hath not God chosen the poor of this world rich in faith, and heirs of the kingdom which he hath promised to them that love him?*
> *6 But ye have despised the poor. Do not rich men oppress you, and draw you before the judgment seats?* (James 2:1-6)

In 1956, a man named Dawson Trotman drowned saving someone else from drowning. Dawson Trotman founded the Navigators, a Christian mission organization, in 1933. Due to the work of the Navigators there were hundreds of saved men on the Navy ships of World War II. If you use the word "discipling" or "disciple" (as a verb), it is because of the movement Dawson Trotman started by the grace of God. There is a story about him. He walked into a fellowship meeting one evening. There were a number of leaders there and many of us would have gone straight to them so we could hobnob with the mighty ones. Not so with Dawson. He noticed a neglected person in a wheelchair nearby. He went straight to that person *first* to show love. Dawson was like that. It is an example for us all.

"*Be not wise in your own conceits*" (v. 16). This phrase is used six times in Scripture: Proverbs 25:26:5, 12, 16; 26:11; Romans 11:25; and here. The word "conceit" here does not mean a proud person, although it is a description of the attitude of someone who is undoubtedly proud. The word means, "Opinion; notion; fancy;

imagination; fantastic notion; as a strange or odd conceit."[47] This person is a very wise person *in his own fantasy*. One of the best commentaries on this phrase was given by Isaiah, "Wo unto them that are wise in their own eyes, and prudent in their own sight" (Is. 5:21). In the context of loving relationships among Christians, don't think of yourselves as too good or too wise to associate with *those* people.

Have Proper Attitudes Toward the Lord

"Not slothful in business" (v. 11) is a command that goes beyond doing a good days work as an employee. It certainly includes that, but the meaning of the word business is not limited to employment or commercial enterprise. One definition of business is, "Something to be done; employment of importance to one's interest, opposed to amusement; as, we have no business in town." [48] This can include any concerns that we need to take care of. We know that "slothful" means "lazy." Scripture tells us, "And whatsoever ye do, do it heartily, as to the Lord, and not unto men" (Col. 3:23).

Be *"fervent in spirit; serving the Lord"* (v. 11). We get our word *zeal* from the Greek word translated *fervent*. The definition of "fervent" includes such things as passionate, engaged, earnest, and excited as well as zealous. [49] The "heartily" in Colossians 3:23 fits well. It is fitting for the phrase "serving the Lord" to follow. Serving the Lord is to be with a fervent heart and in no way slothful. Hence, we speak of being "on fire for the Lord." Jesus spoke of this to the Laodicean church in Revelation.

> *15 I know thy works, that thou art neither cold nor hot: I would thou wert cold or hot.*
> *16 So then because thou art lukewarm, and neither cold nor hot, I will spue thee out of my mouth.*
> *17 Because thou sayest, I am rich, and increased with goods, and have need of nothing; and knowest not that thou art wretched, and miserable, and poor, and blind, and naked:*
> *18 I counsel thee to buy of me gold tried in the fire, that thou mayest be rich; and white raiment, that thou mayest be clothed, and that the shame of thy nakedness do not appear; and anoint thine eyes with eyesalve, that thou mayest see.*
> *19 As many as I love, I rebuke and chasten: be zealous therefore, and repent.* (Rev. 3:15-19)

Rejoicing in hope (v. 12): we looked at the Christians hope in chapters three and four. Our hope includes Christ's second coming, our resurrection, and our inheritance. This is our future. It would only be natural for us to be happy about it. Where is your heart? Is it in Heaven and centered on the Lord? Or, is it on this earth? "If ye then be risen with Christ, *seek those things which are above*, where Christ sitteth on the right hand of God. *Set your affection on things above, not on things on the earth.* For ye are dead, and your life is hid with Christ in God. When Christ, who is our life, shall appear, then shall ye also appear with him in glory" (Col. 3:1-4).

Being patient in trouble (v. 12) is a very difficult thing to do. *Tribulation* is "Severe affliction; distresses of life;

vexations. In Scripture, it often denotes the troubles and distresses which proceed from persecution." [50] The way to deal with tribulation is *patience*, which means the "suffering of afflictions, pain, toil, calamity, provocation or other evil, with a calm, unruffled temper; endurance without murmuring or fretfulness." [51] A person can exhibit patience for many reasons, but in this case it is because of submission to God's will and trust in him. "Thou wilt keep him in perfect peace, whose mind is stayed on thee: because he trusteth in thee. Trust ye in the LORD for ever: for in the LORD JEHOVAH is everlasting strength" (Is. 26:3-4). One reason for tribulation is to teach us the habit of patient trusting in the Lord in all kinds of trouble. Jesus said, "In your patience possess ye your souls" (Luke 21:19). God has made a promise to us in 1 Corinthians 10:13 that makes patience worthwhile: "There hath no temptation taken you but such as is common to man: but God is faithful, who will not suffer you to be tempted above that ye are able; but will with the temptation also make a way to escape, that ye may be able to bear it." Today, our word *temptation* means and enticement to evil. Not so in the time of the KJV translation. It also very often means *trials*. The Greek word used here also means both. This is a promise of God that our patience in trials and enticements will be rewarded.

Continuing instant in prayer completes the triplet of verse 12. Jesus told the story of the woman and the unjust judge in Luke 18. The judge cared for no one, but the woman troubled him with her request so often that he finally granted it. If an unjust uncaring judge would grant the request for someone who continually troubled him, how much more eager is our heavenly father to grant our requests? Jesus told this parable to teach that "men ought always to pray, and not to faint" (Luke 18:1; see 1 Thess. 5:17).

Vengeance is Forbidden
(Rom. 12:14, 17-21)

There are guidelines on how to treat your enemies. To bless those who do you wrong (v. 14) is repeated several times in the New Testament. It is found in Mt. 5:44, "I say unto you, Love your enemies, bless them that curse you, do good to them that hate you, and pray for them which despitefully use you, and persecute you." The Lord Jesus prayed for those who put him on the cross (Luke 23:34). The same sentiment is repeated in Romans 12:20, "Therefore if thine enemy hunger, feed him; if he thirst, give him drink: for in so doing thou shalt heap coals of fire on his head."

When you are wronged by someone the immediate response is usually anger, resentment, or desire for revenge. This is natural for the fallen flesh nature. However, it is contrary to the Spirit of God. These verses absolutely forbid taking vengeance. We are commanded to forgive Christians who wrong us (Eph. 4:31-32). There is nothing in Ephesians 4 that says they must apologize first. The only basis for forgiveness is that Christ forgave us. "Let all bitterness, and wrath, and anger, and clamour, and evil speaking, be put away from you, with all malice: And be ye kind one to another, tenderhearted, forgiving one another, even as God for Christ's sake hath forgiven you." Anger and bitterness are to be replaced with tenderhearted kindness.

The passage in Romans 12 does not limit forgiveness to Christians. When we are wronged, we must let it go. We cannot get revenge and we cannot be glad at any bad thing that happens those who wrong us. "Rejoice not when thine enemy falleth, and let not thine heart be glad when he stumbleth: Lest the LORD see it, and it displease him, and he turn away his wrath from him" (Prov. 24:17-18).

On the contrary, we must not only forgive, but we must bless them and pray for them and, if we have opportunity, do good to them. To do this puts them squarely in the hands of the Lord and He is free to do with them as He pleases. I believe the hope we should have is that God will open their eyes and teach them that what they did was wrong. This, hopefully, will lead them to repentance and a right relationship with God. The *Bible Believer's Commentary; Old and New Testaments* says that we must overcome evil with good:

> 12:20 Christianity goes beyond non-resistance to active benevolence. It does not destroy its enemies by violence but converts them by love. It feeds the **enemy** when he **is hungry** and satisfies his thirst, thus heaping live **coals of fire on his head**. If the live **coal** treatment seems cruel, it is because this idiomatic expression is not properly understood. To heap live **coals** on a person's head means to make him ashamed of his hostility by surprising him with unconventional kindness.
> 12:21 Darby explains the first part of this verse as follows: "If my bad temper puts you in a bad

temper, you have been overcome of evil."

The great black scientist, George Washington Carver, once said, "I will never let another man ruin my life by making me hate him." As a believer he would not allow evil to conquer him. **But overcome evil with good**. It is characteristic of Christian teaching that it does not stop with the negative prohibition but goes on to the positive exhortation. **Evil** can be overpowered **with good**. This is a weapon we should use more frequently.

Stanton treated Lincoln with venomous hatred. He said that it was foolish to go to Africa in search of a gorilla when the original gorilla could be found in Springfield, Illinois. Lincoln took it all in stride. Later Lincoln appointed Stanton as war minister, feeling that he was the most qualified for the office. After Lincoln was shot, Stanton called him the greatest leader of men. Love had conquered! [52]

The Believer and Government
(Rom. 13:1-7)

1 Let every soul be subject unto the higher powers. For there is no power but of God: the powers that be are ordained of God.

2 Whosoever therefore resisteth the power, resisteth the ordinance of God: and they that resist shall receive to themselves damnation.

3 For rulers are not a terror to good works, but to the evil.

Wilt thou then not be afraid of the power? do that which is good, and thou shalt have praise of the same:
4 For he is the minister of God to thee for good. But if thou do that which is evil, be afraid; for he beareth not the sword in vain: for he is the minister of God, a revenger to execute wrath upon him that doeth evil.
5 Wherefore ye must needs be subject, not only for wrath, but also for conscience sake.
6 For for this cause pay ye tribute also: for they are God's ministers, attending continually upon this very thing.
7 ¶Render therefore to all their dues: tribute to whom tribute is due; custom to whom custom; fear to whom fear; honour to whom honour.

This passage calls on "every soul" to submit to "the higher powers." These higher powers are obviously governments. The Roman government was a worldly government that crucified Christ. Notwithstanding, Paul called on believers to submit to it and obey it. So does Peter, "Submit yourselves to every ordinance of man for the Lord's sake: whether it be to the king, as supreme; Or unto governors, as unto them that are sent by him for the punishment of evildoers, and for the praise of them that do well" (1Peter 2:13-14). Along with the call to submit ther are some principles that define God's purpose for governments.

The first principle is that "the powers that be are ordained of God" (Rom. 13:1). We may not like the current government or the current President, but we had better submit because the current government is of God. God is the power above all and every other power exists by His choice and permission. You may not understand why we have the current government, but you must "Trust in the LORD with all thine heart; and lean not unto thine own understanding" (Prov. 3:5). Someone once said that he believed God gave people the government they need and deserve. If society can govern itself, it may get a government that grants liberty. However, if a society cannot govern and control itself, it may get a dictatorship or some other government with great power and control.

The second principle is that if we resist the power, we are resisting God (Rom. 13:2). This is clearly logical if God has ordained the government we are under. Paul never encouraged Christians or Jews to rebel against Rome at any time. He wished Christians to submit, let their light shine in darkness, and glorify God. The focus of Christians is primarily the glory of God in the midst of society, not the betterment of government or culture. This is not to say that a Christian should not seek to influence his government or to enter government service or to right society's wrongs. It is to say that if he does this, his first responsibility is to glorify God in all his efforts (1 Cor. 10:31). The glory of God and the betterment of society is affected by three primary things: follow Christ in all we do, win souls and teach them to follow Christ, and love your neighbor as yourself.

There is an exception to the submission principle. The *Bible Believer's Commentary* explains it this way:

> There is an exception, of course. A Christian is not required to obey if the government orders him to sin or to compromise his loyalty to Jesus Christ (Acts 5:29). No government has a right to

command a person's conscience. So there are times when a believer must, by obeying God, incur the wrath of man. In such cases he must be prepared to pay the penalty without undue complaint.[53]

The third principle is that the purpose of government is to execute punishment on evil doers (Rom. 3:3-4). This necessarily includes two realms, national defense and law enforcement. Evil doers come in two sizes. The first is criminals within the jurisdiction of the government and the second is invaders from outside the jurisdiction, from across the borders. The government, then, should provide domestic tranquility and border security. Regarding border security, it is irrelevant whether they station police, special agents, or the military on the border. The important thing is to keep anyone from crossing the border illegally. God has left the amount of force to be used up to the government involved. Deadly force is permitted under the Noahic Covenant against murderers (Gen. 9:6).

Law enforcement within the borders of the country, which is the jurisdiction of the government, requires that laws be passed first. These laws are to be for the welfare of the people, because the government leader "is the minister of God to thee for good" (Rom. 13:4). Since God calls law breakers "evil doers" and in God's view "evil doers" are also those who transgress His moral laws, man's law should be based on Biblical morality. The laws would be to prevent things from murder and rape to corruption in government and business. They would be laws about problems like theft, fraud, and liable. They would also include laws against government abuse. The loss of life, liberty and property by other people or the government without due process of law amounts to murder and theft. Certainly, all these laws should be based on the truths of the word of God. Since, the good of people requires certain rights, the government should guarantee those rights. These include the right to believe, worship, and practice religion freely. Rights also include the ability to speak and communicate and express one's opinion freely. They include the right to protect yourself, your family, and your property. Therefore, the government must give the people the right to keep and bear arms. There are many more things that could be named here.

Creating laws is followed by detecting and punishing violations of law. Government is usually fairly good at law enforcement and defense, but not much else. The God-given responsibilities of government *do not include* social programs, social welfare, and social health care. The purpose of government is to provide safety and an orderly society for its citizens. To this end, we are to pray for government leaders: "I exhort therefore, that, first of all, supplications, prayers, intercessions, and giving of thanks, be made for all men; For kings, and for all that are in authority; that we may lead a quiet and peaceable life in all godliness and honesty" (1 Tim. 2:1-2).

The fourth principle is that we must submit to government for conscience sake (Rom. 13:5). There are two reasons to submit to government. The first is because, if we do not, we will get in trouble with the power. The second is that it is God's will and command. It will displease Him and hurt our conscience before God. [54]

The fifth principle is that we must pay our taxes and anything else we owe (Rom. 13:6-7). We must pay what we owe. If we owe taxes, we must pay taxes (tribute and customs). However, the office held by government officials also requires the payment of honor, whether we *like* or *agree* with the particular official or not.

Love Fulfills the law
(Rom. 13:8-10)

8 Owe no man any thing, but to love one another: for he that loveth another hath fulfilled the law.
9 For this, Thou shalt not commit adultery, Thou shalt not kill, Thou shalt not steal, Thou shalt not bear false witness, Thou shalt not covet; and if there be any other commandment, it is briefly comprehended in this saying, namely, Thou shalt love thy neighbour as thyself.
10 Love worketh no ill to his neighbour: therefore love is the fulfilling of the law.

The only thing we will never fully be able to pay is love. Once we pay love to others, we immediately owe it again. The list of the commandments in verse nine are the commandments that center on relationships with other people. That's why it says that love is the fulfilling of the law. These commandments define love for your neighbor. If we ever find ourselves faced with a moral decision and we don't know the Biblical answer, opt on the side of love. In order to make sure we can do that, we must be familiar with the definition of love as contained in 1 Corinthians 13:4-8.

4 Charity suffereth long, and is kind; *charity envieth not; charity vaunteth not itself, is not puffed up,*
5 *Doth not behave itself unseemly, seeketh not her own, is not easily provoked, thinketh no evil;*
6 *Rejoiceth not in iniquity, but rejoiceth in the truth;*
7 *Beareth all things, believeth all things, hopeth all things, endureth all things.*
8 *¶Charity never faileth*

Casting Off the Works of Darkness
(Rom. 13:11-14)

11 ¶And that, knowing the time, that now it is high time to awake out of sleep: for now is our salvation nearer than when we believed.
12 The night is far spent, the day is at hand: let us therefore cast off the works of darkness, and let us put on the armour of light.
13 Let us walk honestly, as in the day; not in rioting and drunkenness, not in chambering and wantonness, not in strife and envying.
14 But put ye on the Lord Jesus Christ, and make not provision for the flesh, to fulfil the lusts thereof.

This passage contrasts the works of darkness or the night with the works of the light or the day. There are certain metaphors being used here. Some of the works that Paul lists are works that are usually done in the darkness of the night: "rioting and drunkenness (wild parties), not in chambering (sexual sin) and wantonness (licentiousness)." However, strife and envying occurs in the day as often as it does in the night. The term *night* is a reference to the works done in this *age*; the age we live in is called *night,* an age of darkness (Jn. 1:5; 3:19; 8:12; 12:35, 45). So, Paul says that the night is far spent and the day is at hand. The righteous works mentioned are pictured as works that are characteristics of an age of day and light. That would be the coming millennial age. In Malachi 4:2, the second coming of Christ is pictured by saying "unto you that fear my name shall the Sun of righteousness arise with healing in his wings." It is not S-O-N but S-U-N of righteousness that arises. The coming of Christ is pictured as the sun rising in the morning of a new day. This is what Paul has in mind in Romans 13:11-14. We are to cast off the works of this dark age and live as if we are in the bright light of that new day.

The Believer's Consideration for Others
(Rom. 14:1-15:7)

Some behaviors, thoughts, and attitudes are clearly right and wrong. We can see these in Scripture. Examples are found in the commandments listed in Romans 13, such as, theft, murder, covetousness, and lying. There are other things that are not so clear and are disputed among Christians. They focus on particular behaviors; some say it is right, others say it is wrong, and sometimes neither can get along with the other.

It seems every generation has its own list of disputed behaviors. At one time in the past it was attending theaters and dances. Very few worry about the movies now, but there are other things to fight over. Years ago a friend of mine went to a fellowship conference in the South. When he came back, I asked him how it was. His answer was to this effect, "They preached on the three cardinal sins: pants on women, long hair on men, and tennis shoes." Reportedly, one pastor had some advice for a new convert at church on a Wednesday night: "My men don't wear blue jeans to church on Wednesday night!"

Receive One Another
(Rom. 14:1-4)

1 Him that is weak in the faith receive ye, but not to doubtful disputations.
2 For one believeth that he may eat all things: another, who is weak, eateth herbs.
3 Let not him that eateth despise him that eateth not; and let not him which eateth not judge him that eateth: for God hath received him.
4 Who art thou that judgest another man's servant? to his own master he standeth or falleth. Yea, he shall be holden up: for God is able to make him stand.

Unfortunately, we tend to judge those who do not agree with our convictions. We even tend to think that those who have the most convictions are the strong ones. That's not so. In Romans 14:1-2 we are introduced to two people. One believes he can eat all things and the other is a vegetarian. The vegetarian is considered weak in the faith. It is not that he is a weak Christian. It is his faith in what he can or cannot do that is weak. His conscience is weak.

These convictions have a tendency to become a new law. We have escaped the tyranny of the Mosaic Law only to become trapped by a new law that is usually created by our leaders. These laws are considered to be of high importance and sometimes they are used as the standard by which we judge the spirituality of others. I spoke on the phone to a brother who was attempting to train a new convert. The convert had been saved only a short time. My friend was dismayed because the new convert had not yet quit smoking. I told him that maybe God had some other things He wanted to work on the convert about first, some things of higher priority to God. A number of years ago at a preacher's conference, a well-known preacher was preaching to the others. In a very emphatic way he said to all the assembled preachers, "You can have all the convictions you want. Just don't force them on me!" These "convictions" become as strong and as oppressive as the Mosaic Law. They literally can become a new law that is not explicitly commanded or even mentioned in Scripture. In this case, as in the case of the Law of Moses, the new law dampens Christian spirit and kills enthusiasm (2 Cor. 3:6). In *Balancing the Christian Life*, page 151, Charles Ryrie says:

> At the very outset, let's clarify some things about law and grace. For one thing, they are antithetical concepts, and that antithesis is vitally related to the Christian life. When Paul answers the question of why sin shall not have dominion over the believer, it is with the statement that we are not under the law but under grace (Rom. 6:14). Here, in relation to our

sanctification, being "under grace" is set in sharp contrast to being "under law." In other words, law and grace in this context seem to be opposites and the only way for a Christian to experience a holy life is by being under grace. [55]

How do we handle these debatable things? It seems that they will always be here. Specific items may arise and then fade off the scene while new ones come up, but there will always be items of this type. Romans 14 puts before us some very specific principles to follow.

The first principle is that we must receive one another (Rom. 14:1). Verse one actually says to receive the one who is weak. Paul assumes that the majority of Christians will have strong faith in regard to doubtful matters. However, if the majority of the church is weak on a certain matter and someone who is strong wishes to come into the fellowship, he also is to be received. The term "receive" means to accept this person into the fellowship of the church.

The second principle is that receiving one another is not to be for the purpose of convincing them to change their conviction (Rom. 14:1), "not to doubtful disputations." The acceptance into the fellowship is to be complete and without conditions in these matters. There can be no intentions to persuade the Christian to change his opinion. The Christian and his opinion must be received. You do not have to agree, but each person can have his own opinion on these doubtful things.

Principle number three is that those who are strong are not to despise those who are weak and those who are weak must not judge those who are strong (Rom. 14:3, 4).

How easy it is to say, "Look at her. She's wearing pants! What a carnal Christian she is!" On the other hand, it is also easy to say, "I can't stand people who want to make women live like they were in 1850!" Both attitudes are S-I-N. They are sin, because God has received both persons. Both are God's servants. Christ is our Master. Each of us is individually responsible to our own master.

The fourth principle is "Let every man be fully persuaded in his own mind" (Rom. 5:5-9).

> 5 One man esteemeth one day above another: another esteemeth every day alike. **Let every man be fully persuaded in his own mind.**
> 6 He that regardeth the day, regardeth it unto the Lord; and he that regardeth not the day, to the Lord he doth not regard it. He that eateth, eateth to the Lord, for he giveth God thanks; and he that eateth not, to the Lord he eateth not, and giveth God thanks.
> 7 For none of us liveth to himself, and no man dieth to himself.
> 8 For whether we live, we live unto the Lord; and whether we die, we die unto the Lord: whether we live therefore, or die, we are the Lord's.
> 9 For to this end Christ both died, and rose, and revived, that he might be Lord both of the dead and living.

The most important thing is for each of us to focus on is to please the Lord. So, when we decide what is right or wrong in a certain behavior, let us do it to please and glorify the Lord. That is the attitude that must be behind everything we do. It must not be to please ourselves. It's not to please others with fear of how they will judge us. Our hearts should be centered on pleasing the one who died for us and rose from the dead.

    Principle five is that we will all give account of ourselves to God (Rom. 14:10-12).

> 10 But why dost thou judge thy brother? or why dost thou set at nought thy brother? for we shall all stand before the judgment seat of Christ.
> 11 For it is written, As I live, saith the Lord, every knee shall bow to me, and every tongue shall confess to God.
> 12 So then **every one of us shall give account of himself to God.**

    There will be a future judgment for all Christians, the Judgment Seat of Christ. This judgment is described in 2 Cor. 5:8-10.

> 8 We are confident, I say, and willing rather to be absent from the body, and to be present with the Lord.
> 9 Wherefore we labour, that, whether present or absent, we may be accepted of him.
> 10 For we must all appear before the judgment seat of Christ; that every one may receive the things done in his body, according to that he hath done, whether it be good or bad.

It is also described in 1 Cor. 3:13-15.

> *13 Every man's work shall be made manifest: for the day shall declare it, because it shall be revealed by fire; and the fire shall try every man's work of what sort it is.*
> *14 If any man's work abide which he hath built thereupon, he shall receive a reward.*
> *15 If any man's work shall be burned, he shall suffer loss: but he himself shall be saved; yet so as by fire.*

Get that. Each of us will give account for *himself, and no one else.* I will not give an account for my weaker or stronger brother, but only for my own use or misuse of my convictions. He will account for himself. It's none of my business then or now. I will have enough trouble dealing with my own conscience and convictions now in this life and giving account for them later. That is all I can handle. Leave the other guy alone!

Principle number six is that we are not to judge one another (Rom. 14:13).

> *13 Let us not therefore judge one another any more: but judge this rather, that no man put a stumblingblock or an occasion to fall in his brother's way.*

Even though the brother with a weak conscience on an activity is considered "weak in the faith," the weaker have a tendency to judge those with a stranger conscience.

For example, a few years ago a number of Christians had a conviction against having a Christmas tree in your house. To them, it was a sin. It was the same about having a television in the home. Others thought it was not a sin to have either a Christmas tree or a TV. Their conscience was stronger. However, it was always those with a weaker conscience that looked down on those who had no convictions about trees and TV. They judged those who had freedom to have the trees and TVs. God says accept one another as brothers and sisters and do not judge one another. Everyman stands or falls to his own master.

Principle number seven is "that no man put a stumblingblock or an occasion to fall in his brother's way" (Romans 14:13-21).

> *13 Let us not therefore judge one another any more: but judge this rather, that no man put a stumblingblock or an occasion to fall in his brother's way.*
> *14 I know, and am persuaded by the Lord Jesus, that there is nothing unclean of itself: but to him that esteemeth any thing to be unclean, to him it is unclean.*
> *15 But if thy brother be grieved with thy meat, now walkest thou not charitably. Destroy not him with thy meat, for whom Christ died.*
> *16 Let not then your good be evil spoken of:*
> *17 For the kingdom of God is not meat and drink; but righteousness, and peace, and joy in the Holy Ghost.*
> *18 For he that in these things serveth Christ is*

> *acceptable to God, and approved of men.*
> *19 Let us therefore follow after the things which make for peace, and things wherewith one may edify another.*
> *20 For meat destroy not the work of God. All things indeed are pure; but it is evil for that man who eateth with offence.*
> *21 It is good neither to eat flesh, nor to drink wine, nor any thing whereby thy brother stumbleth, or is offended, or is*
> *made weak.*

Those with the stronger conscience have responsibilities, too. The most important thing is to love your brother regardless of your opinion on these debatable things (things which are often very non-essential). This is the principle that is given the most space in Romans 14. The most important thing is not that you insist on your rights or your liberties, but that you take care not to damage your brother or sister by the exercise of your liberties. The Book of 1 Corinthians has a concrete example of how this can take place. The situation has to do with eating meat in an idol's temple. Paul has taught that meat is meat and comes from God, even if it was butchered in an idol's temple and dedicated to the idol. It will not hurt you if you eat it.

> *8 But meat commendeth us not to God: for neither, if we eat, are we the better; neither, if we eat not, are we the worse.*
> (1 Cor. 8:8)

However, it may not hurt you to eat the idol's meat, but it may actually hurt your brother. You have the knowledge that the meat sold in the idols temple is nothing more than any other meat. However, your brother may not have that knowledge and he could be harmed when you indulge your liberty. How could this happen?

> *9 But take heed lest by any means this liberty of yours become a stumblingblock to them that are weak.*
> *10 For if any man see thee which hast knowledge sit at meat in the idol's temple, shall not the conscience of him which is weak be emboldened to eat those things which are offered to idols;*
> *11 And through thy knowledge shall the weak brother perish, for whom Christ died?*
> *12 But when ye sin so against the brethren, and wound their weak conscience, ye sin against Christ.*
> *13 Wherefore, if meat make my brother to offend, I will eat no flesh while the world standeth, lest I make my brother to offend.*
> (1 Cor. 8:8-13)

In 1 Corinthians 8, we are told that the stronger person is to curtail his liberty if it will cause the weaker to follow his example. If you do it, you may encourage him to do it too, even though he has a weak conscience. To him it is sin, because his conscience is weak. When you do this, you "wound" their conscience; you have made your "brother to offend" God. You have caused him to "perish," in a sense. His growth is hindered; he has lost fellowship with God; he is made subject to God's discipline. There are also several reasons given in Romans 14:14-21 for being very careful not to damage your brother or sister in Christ by the exercise of your liberty.

1) *"Let not then your good be evil spoken of"* (v. 16). You may deem certain activities to be clean activities, but others may deem them to be sinful. If you are in a group like that you would do well to consider curtailing your liberty. Participation in those activities could ruin your reputation among those Christians and make it impossible to minister to them, to impart your spiritual gift to them. Paul said he was "made all things to all men, that I might by all means save some" (see 1 Cor. 9:15-23).

2) *"For the kingdom of God is not meat and drink; but righteousness, and peace, and joy in the Holy Ghost. For he that in these things serveth Christ is acceptable to God, and approved of men"* (vv. 17-18). Here we have the definition of the "kingdom of God:" righteousness, peace and joy in the Holy Ghost. These are the things that must be the priority focus of our energy and our service. Most of the activities we are talking about in relation to Romans 14 are minor. The things of the Kingdom of God are major. As someone has said, "Major in the majors and minor in the minors!"

3) *"Let us therefore follow after the things which make for peace, and things wherewith one may edify another"* (v. 19). Colossian 3:15-16 says, "And let the peace of God rule in your hearts, to the which also ye are called in one body; and be ye thankful. Let the word of Christ dwell in you richly in all wisdom." Peace can only rule when we

follow the word of God. Peace is to rule in both our hearts and in the church. In fact, if it rules in our hearts, it will rule in the church. It will enable the church to maintain love and unity. Jesus said that by our love and unity, the world will know that Christ is genuine and that we are Christ's disciples (John 13:35; 17:23). So, in the church the priority is peace rather than insistence on our liberties or judging those who disagree with us.

4) *"For meat destroy not the work of God. All things indeed are pure; but it is evil for that man who eateth with offence"* (v. 20). Certain activities have no intrinsic sin or evil about them, but if a person considers them to be evil, they are evil to him. If he participates, he has sinned. If a stronger Christian leads him into the activity, he has caused his brother to sin and has sinned himself.

5) *"It is good neither to eat flesh, nor to drink wine, nor any thing whereby thy brother stumbleth, or is offended, or is made weak"* (v. 21). Be willing to give up a rigid insistence on the free exercise of your liberty. This may be difficult, but it is the will of God.

Five Final Conclusions
(Rom. 14:22-15:7)

22 Hast thou faith? have it to thyself before God. Happy is he that condemneth not himself in that thing which he alloweth.
23 And he that doubteth is damned if he eat, because he eateth not of faith: for whatsoever is not of faith is sin. (Rom. 14:22-23)

Romans 15:1 ¶We then that are strong ought to bear the infirmities of the weak, and not to please ourselves.
2 Let every one of us please his neighbour for his good to edification.
3 For even Christ pleased not himself; but, as it is written, The reproaches of them that reproached thee fell on me.
4 For whatsoever things were written aforetime were written for our learning, that we through patience and comfort of the scriptures might have hope.
5 ¶Now the God of patience and consolation grant you to be likeminded one toward another according to Christ Jesus:
6 That ye may with one mind and one mouth glorify God, even the Father of our Lord Jesus Christ.
7 ¶Wherefore receive ye one another, as Christ also received us to the glory of God.

Finally, Paul draws this discussion to a close in Romans 14:22-15:7 with five final conclusions.

1) The first is to the strong in faith and conscience. If you can exercise your liberty without condemning yourself in your heart, it is a happy situation. However, if liberty must be curtailed take joy in that you are pleasing your Master, the lord Jesus Christ.

2) To the weak, he gives a warning. If you partake of an activity when you're are not sure and certain it is right to do, you are committing sin and the Lord will chasten you.

3) Thirdly, Paul reiterates that the greatest responsibility is on the strong to care for the weak. This is the attitude we should have: we must not seek to please ourselves, but put the edification of others first. This is the

attitude that the Lord Jesus had, as quoted in Ps. 69:9. At this point, he inserts a general principle in Romans 15:4 that we would do well to heed. That which has been written in the Old Testament is good for our learning. We should not ignore the Old Testament in favor of the New. There are many things in the Old Testament that teach and illustrate the principles and truths of the New Testament.

      4) The fourth conclusion, in Romans 15:5-6, emphasizes the necessity for us to be unified in heart and mind in order to glorify God together. To glorify God is the first goal of a Christian (1 Cor. 10:31).

      5) Lastly, Paul restates the command he started with, receive one another.

An Old Conflict
(Rom. 15:8-13)

8 Now I say that Jesus Christ was a minister of the circumcision for the truth of God, to confirm the promises made unto the fathers:
9 And that the Gentiles might glorify God for his mercy; as it is written, For this cause I will confess to thee among the Gentiles, and sing unto thy name.
10 And again he saith, Rejoice, ye Gentiles, with his people.
11 And again, Praise the Lord, all ye Gentiles; and laud him, all ye people.
12 And again, Esaias saith, There shall be a root of Jesse, and he that shall rise to reign over the Gentiles; in him shall the Gentiles trust.
13 ¶Now the God of hope fill you with all joy and peace in believing, that ye may abound in hope, through the power of

the Holy Ghost.

In the light of all the previous discussion in the Book of Romans, there is a deeper reason why Paul says to "receive ye one another." Paul again brings up the old conflict between Jew and Gentile in Romans 15:8-13. We must not only receive the weaker or stronger brother into the fellowship of the church, but Jewish Christians must receive Gentile Christians and vice versa. God is building a new man, a new house (Eph. 2:15, 20-22), by combining saved Jews and saved Gentiles into one body in Christ. He calls this one body *the church* (Eph. 1:22-23; 3:1-7). The fact that the body of Christ consists of Jews and Gentiles is the reason why Paul makes a great effort to help them understand the necessity of receiving one another. The body is a spiritual body only and the outward practice is in the local church. It is there that we are exhorted to receive on another.

Chapter Seven

Personal Notes and Conclusions
Romans 15:14-16:27

*A*nd I myself also am persuaded of you, my brethren, that ye also are full of goodness, filled with all knowledge, able also to admonish one another.
15 Nevertheless, brethren, I have written the more boldly unto you in some sort, as putting you in mind, because of the grace that is given to me of God,
16 That I should be the minister of Jesus Christ to the Gentiles, ministering the gospel of God, that the offering up of the Gentiles might be acceptable, being sanctified by the Holy Ghost. (Rom. 15:14-17)

Paul starts his final conclusion and personal notes with an acknowledgement of the condition of the Romans' spirituality (v. 14). He said they were full of goodness. Jesus told us that "none is good, save one, that is, God." No one has intrinsic goodness; we are all sinners. However, we have Christ in us (Col. 1:27) and we are complete in Him (Col. 2:9-10) and goodness is the fruit of the Spirit of God (Gal. 5:22). We may not be good in an absolute moral sense, but the goodness of God is in us. Paul said the Romans were filled with knowledge. Of course, he meant the knowledge of God, not of all things. Knowledge also comes from God (John 14:26). Knowledge along with wisdom and understanding were major prayer requests Paul made for his converts (Eph. 1:16-18; 3:14-19; Col. 1:9; Phil. 1:9). Finally, the Romans were able to admonish one another. "Admonish" means to warn or gently reprove. [56] Another word used in Scripture to describe how we are to motivate each other is *exhort*, which means to encourage, embolden, cheer, advise. [57] The Scripture says, "And let us consider one another to provoke unto love and to good works: Not forsaking the assembling of ourselves together, as the manner of some is; but exhorting one another: and so much the more, as ye see the day approaching" (Heb. 10:24-25).

Though Paul had this confidence in the Roman Christians, he wrote to them hoping to help further their faith (v. 15). He did this to remind them of the grace of God and to impart some spiritual gift as he said in Romans 1:10-11. By giving them all he could, he would help in their sanctification by the Holy Spirit so that the Gentiles could be presented to Christ in holiness (v. 16). Paul's primary ministry was to the gentiles. He was their apostle, although he always took the gospel first to the Jews (Rom. 1:16).

Where Christ is Not Named
(Rom. 15:17-21)

17 ¶I have therefore whereof I may glory through Jesus Christ in those things which pertain to God.
18 For I will not dare to speak of any of those things which Christ hath not wrought by me, to make the Gentiles obedient, by word and deed,
19 Through mighty signs and wonders, by the power of the Spirit of God; so that from Jerusalem, and round about unto Illyricum, I have fully preached the gospel of Christ.
20 Yea, so have I strived to preach the gospel, not where Christ was named, lest I should build upon another man's foundation:
21 But as it is written, To whom he was not spoken of, they shall see: and they that have not heard shall understand.

Paul explained that his basic plan of ministry was to *preach the gospel where it has not been preached before* (Romans 15:17-21). That was what he did when he started on his first missionary journey in Acts 13. It is what he did when he crossed from Asia Minor into the Greek peninsula in Acts 16. It was what he had in mind for the future as he wrote Romans (v. 24, 28). His next intended step was to take the gospel to Spain.

To preach the gospel to those who have not heard is still a necessary goal. We must take the gospel to all nations (Mt. 28:19-20). What is a nation? Too often we think of Biblical nations as political countries. After all, that is the way the term is most often used today. Biblically, the term does not mean a geopolitical country. The Greek word for nation is *ethnos*. It is the word from which we get our word "ethnic." We would do better thinking of *ethnos* in terms of "The Cherokee Nation," "The Sioux Nation," or "The Shawnee Nation." According to Deuteronomy 4:7-8, Israel was a nation before they conquered the Land of Canaan. Using Israel as an example of a Biblical nation, we can discern the definition of *nation*. A Biblical nation has a *common ancestry* (with Israel it was Abraham, Isaac, and Jacob), a *common language* (Israel spoke Hebrew), and *common laws or culture* (Israel had the Law of Moses). Modern mission leaders call these biblical nations *people groups*.

The *Global Status of Evangelical Christianity May 2014* by the International Mission Board gives us a statistical picture of these People Groups as of 2014. [58]

Total Population of the Earth	6,981,425,805
Total Number of Biblical Nations	11,236
Unreached Nations *	6,536
Population Unreached Nations	3,971,515,855
Last Frontier Nations **	4,496
Population Last Frontier Nations	829,727,155
The Most Utter of the Uttermost ***	1,027
Population Most Utter of Uttermost	40,000,000+

Table 4

*Unreached means they are less than 2% born again
**Last Frontier means from no churches/ Christian resources to *some* Christian resources but no active church planting in the last two years. They are all unreached.
***The Most Utter of the Uttermost is my designation

based on Acts 1:8. They are unreached, less than 2% born again. They have had no church planting efforts in the last two years. They have NO Bible in their language.

With this information, it should be abundantly clear that the day of frontier missions is not over. There is still a need to go where the gospel is not being preached. Let us pray that God will raise up laborers to do this as Jesus taught in Luke 10:2. "Therefore said he unto them, The harvest truly is great, but the labourers are few: pray ye therefore the Lord of the harvest, that he would send forth labourers into his harvest."

> ¶For which cause also I have been much hindered from coming to you.
> 23 But now having no more place in these parts, and having a great desire these many years to come unto you;
> 24 Whensoever I take my journey into Spain, I will come to you: for I trust to see you in my journey, and to be brought on my way thitherward by you, if first I be somewhat filled with your company.
> 25 But now I go unto Jerusalem to minister unto the saints.
> 26 For it hath pleased them of Macedonia and Achaia to make a certain contribution for the poor saints which are at Jerusalem.
> 27 It hath pleased them verily; and their debtors they are. For if the Gentiles have been made partakers of their spiritual things, their duty is

also to minister unto them in carnal things.

28 When therefore I have performed this, and have sealed to them this fruit, I will come by you into Spain.

29 And I am sure that, when I come unto you, I shall come in the fulness of the blessing of the gospel of Christ.

This determination to preach Christ where He had not been preached was the main hindrance Paul encountered in getting to Rome (v. 22). Obviously, Rome was a city where Christ was being preached. However, it had come to a point where Christ was generally known in the larger cities all around the eastern Mediterranean coasts and Paul felt he had no more place in those areas (v. 23). So, he had made a new plan, to carry the gospel into Spain. He planned to see the Romans on his way there and hoped to be "brought on his way" by them; that is, he expected to gain some financial support that would help him preach the gospel in Spain (v. 24). First, though, he was going to Jerusalem to take the "poor saints" there an offering that he had gathered from the churches of Macedonia and Achaia (v. 25-27; 1 Cor. 16:1-4; 2 Cor. 8). Along with Paul's statements about his future plans, verse 27 teaches that if someone ministers to our spiritual needs, it is our obligation to minister to their financial and material needs ("carnal things"). The same principle is mentioned in Galatians 6:6, "Let him that is taught in the word communicate unto him that teacheth in all good things." This principle is why missionaries and pastors should be paid so they can attend to the work without distraction (1 Cor. 9:6-14).

Romans 15:30-33 contain three prayer requests from Paul: 1) that he would be delivered from the unbelievers in Jerusalem, 2) that the saints in Jerusalem would accept his offering, and 3) that God would grant that he could travel to Jerusalem and see the saints there.

> 30 ¶Now I beseech you, brethren, for the Lord Jesus Christ's sake, and for the love of the Spirit, that ye strive together with me in your prayers to God for me;
> 31 That I may be delivered from them that do not believe in Judaea; and that my service which I have for Jerusalem may be accepted of the saints;
> 32 That I may come unto you with joy by the will of God, and may with you be refreshed.
> 33 Now the God of peace be with you all. Amen.

God answered all three prayers, but not as Paul expected. Regarding the first, he was delivered from the unbelievers in Jerusalem. They did not raise accusations or arrest him. However, his Jewish enemies from Asia (Asia Minor today) were in Jerusalem and saw him. They raised a huge uproar and it took Roman soldiers to save him (Acts 21:27-40; 22:24). The second prayer was answered, because the saints in Jerusalem peaceably accepted his offering. The third prayer was answered two years later as Paul was carried to Rome as part of a band of prisoners guarded by Roman soldiers. In the mean time he had been kept in Caesarea by the Roman governor. Paul made it to Rome, but as a prisoner. He was held there two years awaiting trial before Caesar. This narrative is found in Acts 22-28.

> Romans 16:1 *I commend unto you Phebe our sister, which is a servant of the church which is at Cenchrea:*
> *2 That ye receive her in the Lord, as becometh saints, and that ye assist her in whatsoever business she hath need of you: for she hath been a succourer of many, and of myself also.*
> *3 Greet Priscilla and Aquila my helpers in Christ Jesus:*
> *4 Who have for my life laid down their own necks: unto whom not only I give thanks, but also all the churches of the Gentiles.*
> *5 Likewise greet the church that is in their house. Salute my wellbeloved Epaenetus, who is the firstfruits of Achaia unto Christ.*

Romans 16 is full of greetings and recommendations with a few final warnings. He begins by commending Phoebe, a "servant of the church which is at Cenchrea" (v. 1-2). Cenchrea was just south of Corinth. [59] She is said to be someone who helped many including Paul. Apparently she was planning a trip to Rome. Paul doesn't say if it was business, ministry, or pleasure, but it is likely that he sent the Book of Romans with her when she left. In the remainder of the chapter there are some other familiar names in the middle of many unfamiliar names. He greets Aquila and Pricilla (v. 3-5). Paul first met them in Corinth (Acts 18), after they had recently arrived there from Rome, and they immediately became ministry partners. When Paul left to return to Antioch in Syria, they went with him. Sailing by the coast of Asia, Paul left them in Ephesus (v. 18-19). After Paul departed, they helped Apollos get straight on his doctrine (Acts 18:26). In the intervening years, they apparently returned to Rome. They were likely there when Paul arrived in Rome. They clearly had a large impact on others in these areas and beyond, even to the point of placing their own lives in danger for Paul's sake. Timothy is mentioned (v. 21) and called Paul's workfellow. Gaius v. 23, with whom Paul was lodging, is a name of at least three men in Paul's experience, Gaius of Macedonia (Acts 19:29), Gaius of Derbe (Acts 20:4), and Gaius of Corinth (1 Cor. 1:14). He is most likely referring to the third one in Romans 16.

> *6 Greet Mary, who bestowed much labour on us.*
> *7 Salute Andronicus and Junia, my kinsmen, and my fellowprisoners, who are of note among the apostles, who also were in Christ before me.*
> *8 Greet Amplias my beloved in the Lord.*
> *9 Salute Urbane, our helper in Christ, and Stachys my beloved.*
> *10 Salute Apelles approved in Christ. Salute them which are of Aristobulus' household.*
> *11 Salute Herodion my kinsman. Greet them that be of the household of Narcissus, which are in the Lord.*
> *12 Salute Tryphena and Tryphosa, who labour in the Lord. Salute the beloved Persis, which laboured much in the Lord.*

13 Salute Rufus chosen in the Lord, and his mother and mine.
14 Salute Asyncritus, Phlegon, Hermas, Patrobas, Hermes, and the brethren which are with them.
15 Salute Philologus, and Julia, Nereus, and his sister, and Olympas, and all the saints which are with them.
16 Salute one another with an holy kiss. The churches of Christ salute you.

The descriptive terms associated with many of the names are significant. The terms listed include firstfuits of Achaia (v. 5), laborer (v. 6-labor), fellow prisoners (v. 7), of note among the apostles (v. 7), beloved (v. 8), helper (v. 9), approved (v. 10), and chosen (v. 13). These terms indicate the love and respect Paul has for them. It is not likely that any of those named labored as much as Paul or accomplished what Paul did, but what they did was very important and necessary. Very few will be a Billy Graham or a Billy Sunday or a Dwight Moody. But, those men could have accomplished very little if it were not for the fellow laborers that took care of the small things and won others here and there. The listing of these believers by name reminds us that God knows our names and each of us is important to Him and the service we perform, no matter how small, is important to Him (Mt. 10:29-31; Luke 12:6-7, 32).

There are also a number of times relatives are mentioned. Andronicus and Junia are said to be kinsmen (v. 7); Herodion is a kinsman (v. 11); Rufus is said to be the writer's brother and his mother is mentioned although not named (v. 13); Lucius, Jason, and Sosipater are also kinsmen (v. 21). Verse twenty-one is immediately followed by "I Tertius, who wrote this epistle, salute you in the Lord" (v. 22). Paul obviously dictated this letter to Tertius who wrote it in the manner of a secretary. Were these Paul's relatives or Tertius' relatives? Given the fact that Paul is responsible for the bulk of the greeting, it is likely they are Paul's kinsmen. Some of these names are mentioned elsewhere in Scripture.

> *17 Now I beseech you, brethren, mark them which cause divisions and offences contrary to the doctrine which ye have learned; and avoid them.*
> *18 For they that are such serve not our Lord Jesus Christ, but their own belly; and by good words and fair speeches deceive the hearts of the simple.*
> *19 For your obedience is come abroad unto all men. I am glad therefore on your behalf: but yet I would have you wise unto that which is good, and simple concerning evil.*
> *20 And the God of peace shall bruise Satan under your feet shortly. The grace of our Lord Jesus Christ be with you. Amen.*

Romans 16:17-20 contain some final exhortations and encouragements. First there is a warning regarding those who cause offenses contrary to good doctrine (v. 17-18). As important as unity among believers is (Eph. 4:3), good doctrine must be maintained. In fact, unity is not only based on love, it is also based on good doctrine (Eph. 4:4-7). Offenses and divisions caused by false teaching is the definition of *heresy*. Romans 16:17 says that we are to separate from these and Titus 3:10 says, "A man that is an heretic after the first and second admonition reject; Knowing that he that is such is subverted, and sinneth, being condemned of himself." Anyone like this is self-centered and self-seeking or as Paul says, "For they that are such serve not our Lord Jesus Christ, but their own belly; and by good words and fair speeches deceive the hearts of the simple." (Rom. 16:18). Paul, on the other hand, is convinced that the Roman Christians are not like this, but have a reputation for being obedient. He, therefore, is glad for them. "I am glad therefore on your behalf: but yet I would have you wise unto that which is good and simple concerning evil" (v. 19). The word "simple," in both verses eighteen and nineteen, means innocent or without guile. [60] Both words apply in regard to a Christian's relationship with evil. The heretics are called deceivers (v. 18) and Satan is called a liar and the Father of it (John 8:44; 2 Cor. 4:4). In verse twenty, Paul seems to connect the deceptive activities of the heretics with Satan, who had no doubt deceived them and was then leading them to attack the Roman church. So, Paul, by the Holy Spirit, promised them quick victory in this battle. May God grant us the same because the deception will get worse (2 Tim. 3:13).

> 21 ¶*Timotheus my workfellow, and Lucius, and Jason, and Sosipater, my kinsmen, salute you.*
> 22 *I Tertius, who wrote this epistle, salute you in*

> the Lord.
> 23 Gaius mine host, and of the whole church, saluteth you. Erastus the chamberlain of the city saluteth you, and Quartus a brother.
> 24 The grace of our Lord Jesus Christ be with you all. Amen.
> 25 ¶Now to him that is of power to stablish you according to my gospel, and the preaching of Jesus Christ, according to the revelation of the mystery, which was kept secret since the world began,
> 26 But now is made manifest, and by the scriptures of the prophets, according to the commandment of the everlasting God, made known to all nations for the obedience of faith:
> 27 To God only wise, be glory through Jesus Christ for ever. Amen. <<Written to the Romans from Corinthus, and sent by Phebe servant of the church at Cenchrea.

Paul closes the Book of Romans in verses twenty-five through twenty-seven by leading them to anticipate further teaching that will reveal truth kept secret since the foundation of the world. This "mystery" is revealed in the Book of Ephesians. We close with these words of William Newell.

> He has been writing with the hand of the Spirit upon him, those stupendous truths which we find in this great, fundamental Epistle: the glory, holiness, and righteousness, of the infinite,

eternal God; the awful guilt and helplessness of man; the story of the astonishing intervention of a Grace that not only pardoned and justified, but made believing sinners partakers in Christ of the very glory of God Himself; the absolute consistency of all this with God's promises to His earthly nation, Israel; the openness of all Heaven now to all nations, and that on the simplest possible condition--Faith alone! And the Apostle has God in view as the Giver, Christ in view as the means, and the saints in view as the receivers of this mighty bounty!

Therefore this great passage becomes both a doxology, and a commendation with a doxology, of praise to this great God, and a commendation of the saints unto Him. Paul thus commended the saints in Ephesus (Act 20:32), "And now, brethren, I commend you to God, and to the Word of His grace." [61]

Afterword

Predestination and Election
Romans 8 and Ephesians 1

*F*or ***whom he did foreknow, he also did predestinate to be conformed to the image of his Son***, *that he might be the firstborn among many brethren.*
30 Moreover whom he did predestinate, them he also called: and whom he called, them he also justified: and whom he justified, them he also glorified. (Rom. 8:29-30)

*4 According as **he hath chosen us** in him before the foundation of the world, that we should be holy and without blame before him in love:*
*5 **Having predestinated us** unto the adoption of children by Jesus Christ to himself, according to the good pleasure of his will,*
*6 **To the praise of the glory of his grace**, wherein he hath made us accepted in the beloved. (Eph. 1:4-5)*

Many commentators equate these verses with the teaching of John Calvin (1509-1564) on *unconditional election*. A simple statement of the doctrine of unconditional election is this: *In eternity past, before the foundation of the world, God knew everyone who would ever live and out of these He arbitrarily chose some to be saved, whom He predestinated to salvation. This choice is called election and it was not based on foreknowledge nor on any good deed or choice the chosen one would ever make. It was not based on foreseen faith on the part of the chosen one.* Other related doctrines of Calvinism are Total Inability (people are completely depraved and unable to choose God or salvation or any spiritual good), Limited Atonement (Christ died for the elect only), Irresistible Grace (some call it the "effectual call"-When God calls you to Himself you cannot resist, i.e. God makes you choose Him), and Perseverance of the Saints (eternal Security). Together these are called *Calvinism* or *Sovereign Grace* or *the doctrines of grace*. Unconditional election is the teaching that before the foundation of the earth, in eternity past, God chose certain people to be saved and left the rest to remain unsaved. The motive for this choice was entirely in the good pleasure of God's will and not because of some merit, choice, or faith He foresaw in those chosen.

It is usually assumed that God's choice (or "election" as it is translated elsewhere) in Ephesians 1:4 and Romans 8:29 is a choice and a predestination *to salvation*.

> Election, according to Calvinism, is God's choice of certain persons for his special favor. ... The sense that primarily concerns us here, however,

is the choice of certain persons to be God's spiritual children and thus recipients of eternal life. [62]

Election is sometimes referred to as *predestination* and *foreordination*. The 1689 Baptist Confession puts it this way in chapter three paragraph three:

> By the decree of God, for the manifestation of His glory, some men and angels are predestinated, or foreordained to eternal life through Jesus Christ ... to the praise of His glorious grace ... others being left to act in their sin to their just condemnation, to the praise of His glorious justice. [63]

Once again, the teaching of unconditional election is God chose only a few (not all) to be saved. The rest (the majority) are left to remain unsaved and go to hell. They call this "grace." John Calvin said it plainly:

> By predestination we mean the eternal decree of God, by which he determined with himself whatever he wished to happen with regard to every man. All are not created on equal terms, but some are preordained to eternal life, others to eternal damnation; and, accordingly, as each has been created for one or other of these ends, we say that he has been predestinated to life or to death. [64]

It has been emphasized that the Bible never says the non-elect are predestined to go to Hell. I wholeheartedly agree with this. The Scriptures never declare that. However, if God has arbitrarily, before the foundation of the world, chosen some (and *only* some) to be saved and go to Heaven, then He has automatically left others to go to the only place they can, Hell. All must go either to Heaven or Hell. There is no other alternative. If the door is shut to Heaven, the non-elect have only one other destiny possible, to go to hell. According to predestination theologians, God alone made that decision. This is the simple reality of the doctrine.

Another related matter is the doctrine of *the sovereignty of God.* This is a key doctrine (perhaps *the* key doctrine) in Calvinistic teaching. Dr. Erikson, in *Christian Theology*, explains this:

> Calvinism's second major concept is the sovereignty of God. He is the creator and Lord of all things, and consequently he is free to do whatever he wills. He is not subject to or answerable to anyone. Humans are in no position to judge God for what he does ... This concept of the divine sovereignty, together with human inability, is basic to the Calvinistic doctrine of election. Without these two concepts the remainder of the doctrine makes little sense. [65]

It is readily admitted that God is sovereign and that all He does is according to the good pleasure of His own will

(Eph. 1:5). However, God's sovereignty is only one of His many attributes and all His attributes work together in perfect harmony. God is not only sovereign and almighty; He is all-knowing, just, holy, gracious, kind, merciful, longsuffering, and wise (Is. 40:28; Job 37:16; 1 John 3:20; Ps. 145:17; Jer. 12;1; Ps. 99:9; 1 Pet. 1:15-16; Ps. 103:8; 2 Pet. 3:9; Rom. 11:33). God is also *love* (1 John 4:8-16). God's will is not arbitrary. God will do all His pleasure (Is. 46:9-10), but when His will operates it is not separated from all that He is. For example, His will operates in all His wisdom and counsel (Eph. 1:7-9, 11). His will is never arbitrary or based on a whim bent to accomplish His pleasure. God's attributes are in perfect balance. God is just. Therefore, our sovereign God can justly condemn all mankind. So, if he chooses the majority to go to Hell, He is just. However, His justice is balanced by His love and mercy. His justice directs wrath toward *all* His creatures, but His love causes Him to direct mercy toward *all* His creatures. We shall see this shortly.

Total Inability

1 And you hath he quickened, who were dead in trespasses and sins;
2 Wherein in time past ye walked according to the course of this world, according to the prince of the power of the air, the spirit that now worketh in the children of disobedience:
3 Among whom also we all had our conversation in times past in the lusts of our flesh, fulfilling the desires of the flesh and of the mind; and were by nature the children of wrath, even as others. (Eph. 2:1-3)

Dr. Erikson said that the sovereignty of God and the doctrine of the inability of man are the two foundational doctrines of Calvinism. He further said that the rest of the so-called doctrines of grace make little sense without them. Having briefly discussed the sovereignty of God, let's take a look at this doctrine of inability. It used to be called "total depravity." This is a new name, but the same doctrine. The doctrine of the inability of man basically states the man is dead in trespasses and sins and a dead man cannot make choices, therefore a man dead in sin cannot make any good spiritual choices. So, an unsaved person *cannot* choose Christ and *cannot* repent of his sins. God must do it in him without any effort from the person himself. This latter operation is called *irresistible grace* or the *effectual call*. Without the doctrine of inability, the doctrine of irresistible grace and the effectual call is an unnecessary doctrine.

It is a true statement that all saved individuals, prior to being born again (John 3:3-6; Titus 3:5), were dead in trespasses and sins. What does this mean? When we see someone who is physically dead, his body cannot move, see, hear, think, speak, reason, make decisions, or do anything else. This is the way some view the meaning of the phrase "dead in trespasses and sins." Augustine (354-430 A. D.), John Calvin (1509-1564 A. D.), and their followers teach that free will is included as dead in this description and every individual is completely unable to make any spiritually good decision. The 1689 Baptist Confession of Faith, Chapter Nine paragraph three, puts it this way:

> Man, by his fall into a state of sin, has wholly lost all ability of will to any spiritual good

> accompanying salvation ... so as a natural man, being altogether averse from that good, and dead in sin, ... is not able by his own strength to convert himself, or to prepare himself thereunto." ⁶⁶

"Dead in sin" means in part that man has "wholly lost all ability of will to choose any spiritual good ..." according to this quote. On the other hand, there were those who had a different opinion. The following quotes are from the early "church fathers" and show that many of them believed in free will, even Ignatius, whose life overlapped that of the Apostles Paul and John. Emphasis in these quotes is mine.

> Seeing, then, all things have an end, and there is set before us life upon our observance [of God's precepts], but death as the result of disobedience, and every one, *according to the choice* he makes, shall go to his own place, let us flee from death, and *make choice of life.* - **Ignatius (35-107)** ⁶⁷
> And again, unless the human race has the power of avoiding evil and choosing good by *free choice, they are not accountable for their actions*, of whatever kind they be. But that it is by *free choice* they both walk uprightly and stumble, we thus demonstrate-**Justin Martyr (110-165)** ⁶⁸
> But this we assert is inevitable fate, that they *who choose the good* have worthy rewards, and they who *choose the opposite* have their merited

awards. For not like other things, as trees and quadrupeds, which cannot act by choice, did God make man: for neither would he be worthy of reward or praise *did he not of himself choose the good*, but were created for this end; nor, if he were evil, would he be worthy of punishment, not being evil of himself, but being able to be nothing else than what he was made. **Justin Martyr (110-165)** [69]

This expression [of our Lord], "How often would I have gathered thy children together, and thou wouldest not," set forth the *ancient law of human liberty, because God made man a free [agent] from the beginning*, possessing his own power, even as he does his own soul, to obey the behests (*ad utendum sententia*) of God *voluntarily, and not by compulsion of God*. For there is no coercion with God, but a good will [towards us] is present with Him continually. And therefore does He give good counsel to all. And *in man, as well as in angels, He has placed the power of choice* (for angels are rational beings), so that those who had yielded obedience might justly possess what is good, given indeed by God, but preserved by themselves. - **Iranaeus (120-202)** [70]

Foolish heretic, who treat with scorn so fine an argument of God's greatness and man's instruction! God put the question with an appearance of uncertainty, in order that even here He might prove man to be the subject of a *free will* in the alternative of either a denial or a confession, and give to him the opportunity of freely acknowledging his transgression ... **Tertullian (145-220)** [71]

Evil had no existence from the beginning, but came into being subsequently. *Since man has free will*, a law has been defined *for his guidance* by the Deity, not without answering a good purpose. For if man did not possess the *power to will and not to will*, why should a law be established? For a law will not be laid down for an animal devoid of reason, but a bridle and a whip; whereas to man has been given a precept and penalty to perform, or for not carrying into execution what has been enjoined. For man thus constituted has a law been enacted by just men in primitive ages. Nearer our own day was there established a law, full of gravity and justice, by Moses, to whom allusion has been already made, a devout man, and one beloved of God. - **Hippolytus (170-236)** [72]

Man was made in the image of God (Gen. 1:27). The image is not a *physical* image, because "God is a spirit" (John 4:24). The image of God probably means many things, such as, knowledge (Col. 3:10), but one thing it certainly means is that man is a trinity like God is a trinity. "And the very God of peace sanctify you wholly; and I pray God your whole spirit and soul and body be preserved blameless unto the coming of our Lord Jesus Christ" (1 Thess. 5:23). Man is a "living soul," and has a body, a soul, and a spirit. Man is three parts, a trinity, just as God is a trinity. Each part of a human being has its own distinct functions. As we all know, the body has the functions of sight, touch, smell, hearing, and speech. The body enables us to relate to the world around us. There is a corrupt nature in man since the fall and it is connected with our flesh (Rom. 7:18, 23).

The soul of a person has the capacities of *mind* (Josh. 22:5; Ps. 119:20; 139:14; Prov. 16:24; 19:2; 24:14;), *emotion* (Gen. 42:21; Deut. 13:3; Josh. 22:5; Jud. 16:16; 1 Sam. 1:10; Job 10:1; Ps. 11:5; Ps. 35:9; Ps. 42:2; 138:3; Song 3:3; Jer. 31:25), and *will* (Josh. 22:5; 1 Kings 2:4; Job 6:7; 7:15; Ps. 57:1; 63:8; 77:2). The Bible sometimes speaks of the soul in such a way that gives the impression it is the body. For example, Leviticus 7:20 speaks of a soul eating of a sacrifice. However, it is the *person,* body and soul and spirit, which commits an action. The soul considers it and makes the decision and the body does the action. The fact that the soul is a separate part of a human being is illustrated in 1 Kings 17:22, where a child is brought back to life when his soul enters into his body again.

The capacities of the human spirit are found in a relationship to God. Man senses and understands the spiritual by his spirit. The term "spirit" from the Hebrew *ruach* is used in various ways in the Old Testament. It can mean breath (Jer. 14:6; Jud. 15:19), purposelessness or uselessness or vanity (Jer. 5:13; Job 16:3), wind (Ex. 10:13), direction (Jer. 49:36), life in man (Gen. 7:21-22), and mind-set or disposition (Ps. 32:2).[73] "Spirit" is also used for the part of man that relates to God along with the soul (Is. 26:9). When a person dies his spirit returns to God (Eccl. 12:7).

Man was made in the image of God before the fall (Gen. 3) and the Bible says he is *still* in the image of God after the fall. "For a man indeed ought not to cover his head, forasmuch as *he is the image and glory of God*: but the woman is the glory of the man" (1 Cor. 11:7). Notice the use of the present tense. Upon extensive search, I have not found one word in Scripture to indicate that the capacities of the soul (mind, emotions, and will) have been in any way destroyed by the fall of man. It is clear from Ephesians 2:1-3 that the soul of the unsaved is under the domination and influence of the flesh, the world and the devil, but the ability to choose, which God gave Adam, remains an active part of our nature.

So, in what way are we dead? Remember that God said to Adam, "But of the tree of the knowledge of good and evil, thou shalt not eat of it: for *in the day* that thou eatest thereof *thou shalt surely die* (Gen. 2:17). They ate and *that day* they died. In what way did they die? It certainly was not their bodies that died. Neither was it their souls. Their bodies and souls (mind, emotion, and will) continued to function. The answer can be found in considering what part of a person is born again when they receive Christ by faith (John 1:12). Jesus said, *"That which is born of the Spirit is spirit."* So, it was Adam and Eve's *spirits* that died that day. In Eph. 2:1, it is the *spirit* of man that is dead, not his soul or his body. An unsaved man cannot have a relationship with God, but he can still think, feel, make choices, and perform actions.

Death is not the end of consciousness. Yes, the death of the body renders it completely inert, but the soul continues as a thinking being. This is clear from Jesus' story of the rich man and Lazarus (Luke 16:19-31). Death, in its basic definition, is separation. The death of the body is the separation of the body from the soul and spirit. The death of the soul is separation from God (Rev. 20:11-15). The current death of the spirit is separation from the life of God. All death is caused by sin (see Rom. 5; 6:23). That the spirit still has some ability to function is evident from 1 Cor. 2:11: *"For what man knoweth the things of a man, save the spirit of man which is in him?"* The spirit we have in us helps us understand our own life. So "death" does not mean a complete ceasing of function or an end of consciousness or an inability to make decisions, even spiritual ones. It means we are cut off from the life of God, eternal life, and we are separated from Him, without God, and without hope (Eph. 2:11-12).

However, it is clear that when we were unsaved, we were under the domination of sin. Specifically, we were dominated by the flesh, the world (1 John 2:16), and the devil, the prince of the power of the air. The Bible says some harsh things about the condition of mankind. *"All have sinned"* (Rom. 3:26). The lists in Romans 3:10-18 and 1:18-32 present a very dark and bleak picture. The statements of Romans 1:18-28 are clearly general statements about mankind and every sin listed does not apply to every person. Not everyone will be a fornicator or a homosexual. So, the list in Romans 1:29-32 is a general list of sins and activities that will be found among mankind as a whole. The same is true of the list in Romans 3:10-18, although that is not as clear. There are statements, such as, "there is none that seeketh after God" (Rom. 3:11) and "there is none that doeth good, no, not one" (Rom. 3:12) that seem to apply to all. Yet, statements like, "Their feet are swift to shed blood: destruction and misery are in their ways" (Rom. 3:15, 16), clearly do not apply to every individual, because not everyone is swift to shed blood and spread destruction. Some of the statements are quoted from Ps. 14:1-3 and Ps. 53:1-3, both of which are applied to atheists. These statements are general statements that are intended by Paul to convey the utter corruption of the human race as a whole. These verses have been used by Calvinism to teach that human beings are incapable of making any good decisions morally because of the fallen human nature we are born with. However, nearly the entire picture is a picture of behavior after birth; it is not a description of man's basic fallen nature.

Humans are capable of good acts and good decisions, but they cannot be good enough to earn Heaven or match God's goodness. Compared to God's standards, we are not good at all. Jesus said, "If ye then, being evil, *know how to give good gifts* unto your children, how much more shall your Father which is in heaven give good things to them that ask him" (Matt. 7:11)? Giving a good gift to our children is a good act. It does not displease the Lord. There are many such acts that are done every day.

What about spiritual decisions that accompany salvation? Acts 10 introduces Cornelius, a Roman centurion, who is said to be "a devout man, and one that feared God with all his house, which gave much alms to the people, and prayed to God always" (Acts 10:2). This man was not a saved man. He was a sincerely religious man, who did good acts (giving alms). He believed in the God of the Old Testament, but not in Jesus Christ. The Bible gives two evaluations of Cornelius' religious spirit. The first comes from the angel who told him to send for Peter. "And he said unto him, Thy prayers and thine alms are come up for a memorial before God" (Acts 10). God saw and took special positive notice of his actions. God heard the prayers of an unsaved man in that sense (see vv. 30-31). The second is from Peter, "Of a truth I perceive that God is no respecter of persons: but in every nation he that feareth him, and worketh righteousness, is accepted with him" (Acts 10:34-35). I am not saying that Cornelius got to the point he did without the work of the Holy Spirit in his life, but he was not saved; he had not been born again. Yet, he was able to do good acts and he was able to make positive spiritual decisions.

People *can* make spiritual decisions. They *can* repent and come to Christ. The words of the Lord Jesus agree to this. There was a time when Jesus hid His words from a group who were under the judgment of God. In spite of being under God's judgment, these people could evidently choose to receive the truth anyway. Steve Jones, a former Calvinist, explains:

> Jesus himself did not seem to have been a believer in Total Inability. We read in Mark 4:11, 12 that he spoke in parables as a judgment against the obstinate Jews. The purpose of parables was to keep his message from entering their ears, "otherwise they might turn and be forgiven" (v.12). Had those stiff-necked people been allowed to hear the truth straight out, *they might have turned to receive it.* But how?

Calvinism tells us that no one can turn and receive the forgiveness of sins because of Total Inability passed from Adam. There must first be an inward miracle of the heart, an "effectual call." [74]

Total Inability and Salvation

For by grace are ye saved through faith; and that not of yourselves: it is the gift of God: Not of works, lest any man should boast. For we are his workmanship, created in Christ Jesus unto good works, which God hath before ordained that we should walk in them (Eph. 2:8-10).

For the most part, these are very clear verses. Grace gives us salvation. The means grace uses to save us is faith. None of it is from us. It is all from God. It is the gift of God. It is easily understandable that the grace is God's grace, so it cannot in any way be from us. The salvation is entirely of God, because we cannot save ourselves or do anything that earns salvation. How is it that faith is also not of us? God supplies us the faith, but how does He do that? It comes through the Word of God. *"So then faith cometh by hearing, and hearing by the word of God"* (Rom. 10:17). We hear the gospel and it results in faith. On the other hand, the Scriptures command us to believe and tells us that, when someone believes, *"**his** faith is counted for righteousness"* (Rom. 4:5). Therefore, there is also a human element involved. When you got saved, God showed you the truth from the Word of God and the Holy Spirit helped you, so faith originated from God. God enabled you to believe.

However, it was you who believed. Faith, however, is not a good work that earns salvation.

> God justifies the believing man, not for the worthiness of his belief, but for the worthiness of Him in whom he believes" [Hooker]. The initiation, as well as the increase, of faith, is from the Spirit of God, not only by an external proposal of the word, but by internal illumination in the soul [Pearson]. Yet "faith" cometh by the means which man must avail himself of, namely, "hearing the word of God" (Rom_10:17), and prayer (Luk_11:13), though the blessing is wholly of God (1Co_3:6, 1Co_3:7). [75]

Salvation is "not of works, lest any man should boast" (verse 9). If the grace of God that brings salvation is to abound to God's glory (Eph. 1:6; 2:7), then there can be nothing in salvation that can give man reason to boast. When God says this, He is specifically looking at "works." Romans 4:4 says, "Now to him that worketh is the reward not reckoned of grace, but of debt." If a person could work for salvation and earn it, God would owe it to him as a matter of debt. But no one can earn it. No one is good enough to deserve it. "But to him that worketh not, but believeth on him that justifieth the ungodly, his faith is counted for righteousness" (Rom. 4:5). The basis of salvation cannot be both works and grace through faith. "And if by grace, then is it no more of works: otherwise grace is no more grace. But if it be of works, then is it no more grace: otherwise work is no more work" (Rom. 11:6). "Where is boasting then? It is excluded. By what law? of works? Nay: but by the law of faith. Therefore we conclude that a man is justified by faith without the deeds of the law" (Rom. 3:27-28). Whether a person has the ability to make a decision or not, is not part of the question about boasting. God says that a person cannot work for salvation and he cannot save himself, therefore he has no basis for pride or boasting. This concept is also the reason you can be confident that you will never lose your salvation. If you cannot work to get saved, you cannot work to keep your salvation. You are "kept by the power of God through faith" (1 Peter 1:5). Grace saves you and grace keeps you.

So let's try to bring this all together:

1. People are dead spiritually (Eph. 1:1-3)

2. They are dominated and influenced by the flesh, the world, and the devil.

3. Therefore, God had to bring influences of His own to people.

4. The influences from God include illumination (John 1:9), conviction from the Holy Spirit (John 16:7-11), drawing power (John 6:44), the gospel and calling by it (2 Thess. 2:14), and the availability of faith (Rom. 10:17).

5. These influences of God come through the Holy Spirit and the Word of God, making it immensely important that the Word of God be spread across the globe in every language.

Man cannot save himself or earn his salvation, but he can choose whether he will receive Christ or reject Him. "O Jerusalem, Jerusalem, thou that killest the prophets, and stonest them which are sent unto thee, how often would I have gathered thy children together, even as a hen gathereth her chickens under her wings, and **ye would not**" (Matt. 23:37). The Lord was completely sincere in His statement that they could and would have been accepted by Him. He was completely sincere that he desired this. However, they refused. "Ye stiffnecked and uncircumcised in heart and ears, **ye do always resist** the Holy Ghost: as your fathers did, so do ye" (Acts 7:51). Here are people who had the work of the Holy Spirit going on in their hearts. Why did the Holy Spirit work on them if not to bring them to repentance? Yet, they refused. "Search the scriptures; for in them ye think ye have eternal life: and they are they which testify of me. And **ye will not come to me**, that ye might have life" (John 5:39-40). "Come now, and **let us reason together**, saith the LORD: though your sins be as scarlet, they shall be as white as snow; though they be red like crimson, they shall be as wool" (Is. 1:18). "I call heaven and earth to record this day against you, that I have set before you life and death, blessing and cursing: therefore **choose life**, that both thou and thy seed may live" (Deut. 30:19). Could they all choose life or was God just lying? (Moses was speaking God's message under the inspiration of the Holy Spirit.) "And if it seem evil unto you to serve the LORD, **choose you this day** whom ye will serve … but as for me and my house, we will serve the LORD" (Josh. 24:15).

Some point to John 1:12-13 to make the point that man's choice has nothing to do with salvation. "But as many as received him, to them gave he power to become the sons of God, even to them that believe on his name: which were born, not of blood, **nor of the will of the flesh, nor of the will of man**, but of God." However, these verses do not say that man's will has nothing to do with salvation. It says that your choice did not and cannot save you, God alone can do that.

Let's illustrate the matter. Let's suppose a man comes to me and says, "You have a mortgage on your home of $100,000, right?" "Yes," I answer. "Would you like to be free of that debt?" He inquires. Again I answer, "Sure." The man smiles, "I'm going to pay your mortgage for you and you can still own the house." I could look at him, decide he is just teasing me, and decide to reject his offer; or, I could believe him and decide to accept his offer. The choice is mine. If I decide to accept the offer, the man pays my mortgage. Is my freedom from debt my doing? I certainly did not earn it. It was a free gift. Did my will accomplish it? Absolutely not! My freedom from debt was totally of the gracious offer and action of my benefactor. It was not of my will in any way. By refusing the offer, I could have prevented the man from paying my debt. However, my acceptance of the offer accomplished only one thing. It freed the man to do what he had determined to do in the first place, pay my debt. My will did not make me debt free. Could I say, "I made myself debt free" and it be true? I could not. It would be a lie. I could have willed all day and all night and I still would have owed the debt. Only the gracious payment, which my benefactor conceived, offered, and provided, made me debt free. I have nothing to boast of. So, my will cannot save me. Only my Savior can do that. My will may free Him to do it, but my will cannot accomplish it.

Some may say, "You can boast because you had the wisdom to accept his offer. Not so. In regard to accepting

Christ, the wisdom came from the Lord. I was blind and ignorant, but God illuminated my understanding by the wisdom of the gospel. I was faced with a "no brainer." Accept Christ and go to Heaven or reject Christ and go to Hell. God gave me the wisdom of His truth. I have chosen Christ, but it is no glory to me.

"We Take These Truths to be Self-Evident."

These words from the Declaration of Independence remind us that there are certain *unchangeable and inviolate truths* that should be understood and never forgotten. Certain truths of Scripture about God and His plan of salvation fall into this category. Whatever the truth is about election and predestination, it will not contradict certain inviolate truths. These are truths that are absolutely foundational. All truth is rooted in the person and character of God Himself, whether it is election and predestination or love and mercy. God *never* contradicts Himself.

The first thing any doctrine of election cannot contradict is that "God is love." These words from 1 John 4:8 and 16 bring up a subject that God says is "the greatest of these" (1 Cor. 13:13). Love is not simply a characteristic of God. Love is said to be what God *is*. It isn't that love is what God *does* (John 3:16), love is an essential part of God's essence; not just a characteristic of His nature, but it is an essential part of *what* God *is*.

What is love? When John says that God is love (1 John 4:8, 16) he connects the love of God with our Christian love for one another. "Beloved, let us love one another: for love is of God; and every one that loveth is born of God, and knoweth God. He that loveth not knoweth not God; for God is love" (1 John 4:7-8). Jesus said, "Greater love hath no man than this, that a man lay down his life for his friends" (Jn. 15:13). This is the kind of love we are to have for one another. However, it is Jesus Himself (who is God- 1 Tim. 3:16) who truly loved like that. The love we have for the brethren is the same kind of love that God has.

This love that we are to have for one another is described in detail in 1 Corinthians 13, the love chapter. To summarize that chapter, love consists of both attitude and action. The basic truth is that love seeks the good, welfare, and happiness of the objects of love. Since love of one Christian for another is from God, then when God loves, He is doing the same; He seeks the good, welfare, and happiness of those He loves. In the love chapter (1 Cor. 13), it is said, "And now abideth faith, hope, charity (love), these three; but the *greatest* of these is charity." This not only shows what our attitude is to be, but it reveals the attitude of God. He considers love to be greater than faith and hope. Earlier in the chapter, love is compared to speaking in tongues and prophesying. Tongues are exercised only by the power of God and prophecy can only be known by the omniscient revelation of God. God said that anyone doing these things (and they can only do them by the power and sovereign will of God) is *nothing* unless they do them *in love*. *Seeing that this is the attitude of God, it is clear that the good pleasure of His sovereign will is guided by His love.*

Who does God love? Certainly God loves His Son (Mt. 3:17) and His children (John 16:27). Our topic calls for us to examine God's love for sinners. which is revealed in the classic verse, "For God so loved the world, that he gave his only begotten Son, that whosoever believeth in him should not perish, but have everlasting life" (John 3:16). This speaks of God's provision of salvation for all of mankind. John, the Baptist declared of Jesus, "Behold the Lamb of God, which taketh away the sin of the world" (John 1:29). *It cannot be denied that God loved the world.*

However, some have said that "the world" here means *the elect*. From this, they have also taught that Jesus only died for the elect. They call this "limited atonement." God loved the world and Jesus came to take away the sin of the world. What is meant by "the world?" It is true that there are times when the term has a limited or qualified application that is clear from the context, but does it here?

John 3:16 is clearly speaking about God's provision of salvation for *people*. John the Baptist was speaking of Jesus taking away the sin of *people*. So, the focus is on people. In Mark 16:15 Jesus commanded, "Go ye into all the world, and preach the gospel to every creature." The goal of gospel preaching is "all the world" and "every creature." Jesus then is telling them to preach the gospel throughout the world that exists under heaven and to every person who lives there. If the gospel is to be preached to all of them, then it was "every creature" for whom Christ died. Indeed, we find that the Scripture says the same. "And he is the propitiation for our sins: and not for ours only, *but also for the sins of the whole world*" (1 John 2:2). "Propitiation" means that Christ's death satisfied the penalty for sin. "Ours" in this verse refers to believers, the elect. So, let's paraphrase this statement and say, "He is the propitiation for the elect's sins: and not for the elect's sins only, *but also for the sins of the whole world.*" Therefore, God loved the entire world so much that He gave His only begotten Son to die for both the elect and the non-elect, or rather, for those who would accept Him by faith and also for those who would reject Him. The term "world" in John 3:16 should be understood in its normal meaning to include every person in the world past, present, and future; not just the elect. *God loved everyone in the world and Jesus died for everyone ever born in the world, not just those called "the elect."*

The second truth that any doctrine of election cannot contradict is the fact that God desires and wills that everyone be saved. According to unconditional election it is the good pleasure of God's will to save only some people, a remnant out of all mankind, and leave the rest to die in their sins to spend eternity in Hell. This must have been His will if they are right. How many people have lived in all of history? It is unknown, but it must have been many billions. We can tell that because about seven billion are living now. One thing history makes clear is that a minority of people have been saved in every generation. Let's get some idea of the magnitude of what we are saying. How many are saved today? Fifteen percent? Thirty percent? Let's say that a full fifty percent of all people living on earth today are saved. It is probably not near that number in reality. That still leaves fifty percent of them, or about 3 billion 500 million who, according to unconditional election, are not elect and will go to hell by God's good pleasure and grace! That's only among those living today. It doesn't count the six thousand years of human history before today! I say, this is *not God's will!*

How do we know God wishes for everyone to be saved? Simple Scripture, that's how.

1) John 3:16, sets the stage revealing two things: God loved all unsaved human beings and He gave His son to provide for their salvation.

2) "And he said unto them, Go ye into all the world, and preach the gospel to every creature. He that believeth and is baptized shall be saved; but he that believeth not shall be damned" (Mark 16:15-16). Jesus' last command was to preach the gospel to every human being, sincerely inviting all of them to come to the Savior.

3) "No man can come to me, except the Father which hath sent me draw him: and I will raise him up at the last day" (John 6:44). "And I, if I be lifted up from the earth, *will draw all men unto me*" (John 12:32). People cannot come to Christ on their own power. The way the Father enables people to come is to "draw" them. Jesus promised that if He would be lifted up from the earth (crucified, see verse 33), *He would draw everyone.*

4) "... the Comforter ...will reprove the world of sin, and of righteousness, and of judgment: Of sin, because they believe not on me; of righteousness, because I go to my Father, and ye see me no more; of judgment, because the prince of this world is judged" (John 16:7-11). Jesus promised that the Holy Spirit, the Comforter, will convict every person in the entire world of sin, righteousness, and judgment to come.

5) "The same (John the Baptist) came for a witness, to bear witness of the Light, that *all men through him might believe.* He was not that Light, but was sent to bear witness of that Light. That was the true Light, which *lighteth every man that cometh into the world*" (John1:7-9). John came to bear witness of the true Light, Jesus Christ, who lightens

every human who comes into the world. According to Thayer the Greek word for light, *photizei*, in this context means, "To enlighten, spiritually, imbue with saving knowledge." [76] So, it involves spiritual enlightenment given to every single person ever to be born (see Eph. 1:18 for use of the same Greek word). The purpose of this is that *"all men … might believe."*

These verses teach us how God is dealing with each and every sinner. We are commanded to preach the gospel to every individual. He will convict each of them of their sin, the necessity of righteousness, and their judgment to come. Finally, He will draw them each and every one, thereby enabling them to come to Christ and believe. God promises that He will enlighten each of them, thereby helping them understand the gospel. These benefits come to everyone. We may not understand how He does all this, but He does, nonetheless. This is consistent with the fact that He loves all people and wishes them to be saved. In this regard, He still has more to say.

6) "For this is good and acceptable in the sight of God our Saviour; *who will have all men to be saved*, and to come unto the knowledge of the truth (1 Tim. 2:3-4). This is a clear statement that it is God's "will" that "all men" be saved. The Greek word for "will," the verb *thelo*, means "to will, have in mind, intend." [77] The same word in noun form is used in Eph. 1:5, 11, "the good pleasure of his will" and "the counsel of his own will." Do you want to know what the good pleasure of God's will is? The good pleasure of God's will and the counsel of His own will is *that all men be saved and come to the knowledge of the truth!* This is truth that no correct doctrine of election can violate or contradict,

as the doctrine of unconditional election absolutely does. According to God's own statement, if the total inability of man is true and God must so manipulate an elect person that he will be saved regardless of any other factors, then *God would elect all men*, because He wills, has in mind, and intends that they all be saved.

7) "The Lord is not slack concerning his promise, as some men count slackness; but is longsuffering to us-ward, not willing that any should perish, but that all should come to repentance" (2 Pet. 3:9). This does not teach that God is delaying the second coming and the end. What it does say is that God has worked out the timing so that the maximum number will get saved before the end. Why? Because He is *not willing* that *any* should perish. The Greek word for "willing" here is *boulomai* and means "to will deliberately, have a purpose, be minded." [78] According to this definition and 2 Pet. 3:9, God has never had an eternal purpose that anyone should perish. If two people knock on your door in a cold snowy night and you open the door and choose only one to let in to the warm house, you have automatically chosen to allow the other to remain out in the cold. Unconditional election says that God not only does this (some go to Heaven and the rest are left to go to Hell), but that He planned or purposed to do that before the foundation of the world. 2 Pet. 3:9 says that God doesn't do that. *It says that God does not make a deliberate purpose or plan that leaves some to go to hell unconditionally.* The doctrine of unconditional election teaches that He did exactly that.

8) A very good reason for believing that God wants everyone to be saved is *the purpose for which He sent the*

Lord Jesus Christ. Following the very powerful words of John 3:16, we read these words: "For God sent not his Son into the world to condemn the world; but that the world through him might be saved" (John 3:17). For you scholars out there, the Greek words for "that ... might be saved" are *ina sothe*. *Sothe* (might be saved) is in the subjunctive mood. For those of you who do not know what that means, it means, the word expresses a *wish* and a *hope*. It expresses a *distinct possibility.* John Pappas, Th. D., explains it this way in his Greek grammar: "The Greek subjunctive is the mood of possibility ... In grammar it is the mood of uncertainty, a wish, or an uncertain condition ... The subjunctive mood expresses an action which is not really taking place but which is objectively possible." [79] Both the Greek and the English of John 3:17 expresses the possibility that all the world can get saved. They are not all *getting* saved, but they all *can* get saved. It is an *objective possibility.* The presence of *ina* in the Greek text makes the subjunctive a purpose statement. It was God's *purpose* to save everyone in the world through Christ. *That is the reason why He came.* There is no possible way that God limited the number of individuals who could get saved or determined to leave anyone out.

9) Finally, when Paul preached in Athens, he stood on Mars Hill and drew the audience's attention to their rampant idolatry, declaring, "And the times of this ignorance God winked at; but now commandeth *all men every where* to repent" (Acts 17:30). According to Calvinism, people are unable to make any good spiritual decisions. Therefore, only the elect can obey this command. That means God commands all men everywhere to repent, even those who

cannot repent, because God will not enable them to do so. Still, God holds them responsible and punishes them for disobedience. This is a truly twisted theology. The natural and normal interpretation is that if God commanded them to repent, they *can* or He *will enable* them. This command goes out to every individual on earth and that implies that all *can* repent and be saved.

The third truth that no doctrine of election can contradict is that there is no respect of persons with God. The phrase that God does not have "respect of persons" is found in the Bible six times (2 Chron. 19:7; Acts 10:34; Rom. 2:11; Eph. 6:9; Col. 3:25; 1 Pet. 1:17) and others are warned about having respect of persons three times (Prov. 14:23; 28:21; Jas. 2:1). "And if ye call on the Father, who without respect of persons judgeth according to every man's work, pass the time of your sojourning here in fear" (1 Pet. 1:17). God clearly is without respect of persons in judgment. The phrase, "respect of persons," means to show favoritism to some, while taking it away from others. However, God doesn't play favorites. Yet, that's exactly what the doctrine of unconditional election has Him doing and that favoritism is in the area of judgment.

The doctrine of unconditional election, or as some call it "sovereign grace," contradicts each of these truths. God's sovereignty is not the greatest thing about Him, because His sovereign activity is guided by His wisdom, His grace, His loving-kindness, His justice, His mercy, and all His other attributes, especially His love. His love makes Him desire the welfare, good, and happiness of all His created creatures. The doctrine of unconditional election has Him deliberately consigning the vast majority of His human creatures to eternity in Hell with no genuine opportunity to escape it. Yes, He is just and righteous to do so, because of our sin. But, is He loving and merciful to do so? It is because of His love and mercy that He sent His only begotten Son into the world to die for all sinners and provide a way to escape for everyone. God wills that all people be saved. Unconditional election, on the other hand, says that it is His will that only a few be saved and that the rest go to Hell. God does not make a purpose to deliberately unconditionally consign people to Hell. He is not willing that any perish. Yet, unconditional election says He certainly is willing and that it is a purposeful part of His plan. God does not show respect of persons, play favorites, in judgment. He is equally fair in His judgment to all. Yet, unconditional election has him picking favorites, who will be saved, while His rejects will be left to go to Hell. It makes God look like a capricious arbitrary despot. Unconditional election is contrary to the nature and the revealed will of God.

The Real Story

What is election all about, then? The first thing to understand is that the choice spoken of in Ephesians 1:4 *is not a choice to salvation*. The verse clearly says that the goal of the choice is to make us "holy and without blame before Him in love;" Before the foundation of the world, God clearly knew all who would be in Christ. He chose those who would be in Christ to be finally and forever confirmed in holiness and blamelessness. That condition is the goal of the entire Christian life and will ultimately be realized at the second coming. God wants us to strive to be holy and blameless in behavior now (1 Thess. 5:23). But, some verses point to a perfection of holiness as an ultimate end goal of the Christian life. "Who shall also confirm you unto the end, that ye may be blameless in the day of our Lord Jesus Christ" (1 Cor. 1:8).

That this is the view in Eph. 1:4 is confirmed by the connection of election with predestination in verse five, which says, "Having predestinated us unto the adoption of children by Jesus Christ to himself." The key that points to the end of the Christian life is the "adoption of children." The adoption is clearly defined in Scripture: "... ourselves also, which have the firstfruits of the Spirit, even we ourselves groan within ourselves, *waiting* for *the adoption, to wit, the redemption of our body*." The adoption is the redemption of our body, which will take place at the second coming. "Beloved, now are we the sons of God, and it doth not yet appear what we shall be: but we know that, when he shall appear, we shall be like him; for we shall see him as he is" (1 John 3:2). "For our conversation is in heaven; from whence also we look for the Saviour, the Lord Jesus Christ: who shall change our vile body, that it may be fashioned like unto his glorious body, according to the working whereby he is able even to subdue all things unto himself (Phil. 3:20-21).

For those who say we are adopted when we get saved, I have a news flash. We were not adopted into God's family; we were *born* into it (John 3:3-7; 1:12-13). It is our spirits that receive the new birth, because they were dead (John 3:6; Eph 2:1). The new birth does nothing for our bodies. They are not saved yet. The body cannot be born again, so, it must be adopted. We do not yet have the adoption. If we do, why must we *wait* for it? We have the *Spirit* of adoption now (Rom. 8:15), but the adoption itself, or redemption of our bodies, will take place at the rapture, when the church is taken out of the world (1 Thess. 4). This view of adoption also explains the mention of predestination in Rom. 8:28-30. The goal of predestination in those verses is also *not* salvation (in the sense of justification and new birth), but it is to be "conformed to the image of his Son." This will be perfected at the second coming and includes the redemption of the body, in accordance with the verses in 1 John 3:1-3 and Philippians 3:20-21. Therefore, the choice of election and predestination in Eph. 1:4-5 and Romans 8:28-30 focuses on the end of the Christian life, not the beginning.

There is an Election to Salvation

Perhaps the key verses to explain election to salvation are found in 2 Thessalonians 2:13-14.

> But we are bound to give thanks alway to God for you, brethren beloved of the Lord, because **God hath from the beginning chosen you to salvation** through sanctification of the Spirit and belief of the truth: Whereunto he called you by our gospel, to the obtaining of the glory of our Lord Jesus Christ.

The companion verse to these is 1 Peter 1:2: "Elect according to the foreknowledge of God the Father, through sanctification of the Spirit..."

2 Thessalonians 2:13-14 uses a different Greek word for "chosen" than the word in Ephesians 1:4, which uses the Greek word *eklegomai* or (in noun form) *eklektos,* which means *to choose, chosen.* [80] The word in 2 Thessalonians is *aireomai* and it means *to choose.* [81] Some criticize the use of 2 Thessalonians 2:13, because it does not use the word *eklektos.* However, this is a failure to understand language. The two words are synonyms; they both mean *to choose.* A normal characteristic of languages is words that mean the same and are interchangeable. In English it would be proper to say, "He was elected" or to say, "He was chosen." Both are proper and both mean the same. Also, 1 Peter 1:1-2, the companion verse to 2 Thessalonians 2:13, uses the word *eklektos.*

Some will no doubt object to using 2 Thessalonians 2:13-14 to explain election on the basis of context. The context talks about the future tribulation period that will precede the second coming of Christ. He says the antichrist will come ...

> ... *with all deceivableness of unrighteousness in them that perish; because they received not the love of the truth, that they might be saved. And for this cause God shall send them strong delusion, that they should believe a lie: that they all might be damned who believed not the truth, but had pleasure in unrighteousness.* (2 Thess. 2:11-12).

These are people who will perish in the Great Tribulation. Why do they perish? Was it because they were not among the elect? Was it because they were not elect that God will send strong delusion to them that they might believe lie? Their status of being elect or not has nothing to do with it. They will perish, because they had a chance to get saved and refused it. They could have been saved, but they "believed not the truth." They could have "received the love of the truth," but they refused that also. Paul is contrasting the situation of these with the salvation of the Thessalonian Christians. Those who will perish could have believed the truth and gotten saved, but they refused the truth. On the other hand, the Thessalonian Christians were chosen to salvation *because they believed the truth.* The salvation of the Thessalonians was a salvation from the wrath of God in the Tribulation. However, it was more than that. The salvation was received when they were "sanctified by the Spirit." That is, they were saved when they believed the gospel. When we first trust Christ we get a lot of salvation in one big package. Our spirits are born again, our souls are saved, and we have guaranteed salvation of our bodies and salvation from wrath in the coming tribulation. We get it all at once. So, the salvation Paul is talking about in 2 Thessalonians 2:13-14 is that whole package we get the day we receive Christ.

    The verses in 2 Thessalonians clarify the truth about God choosing us to salvation. It is clearly stated, "God hath from the beginning chosen you to salvation." The verses define the timing of the choice, the means by which the choice is made, and the vehicle used to call the sinner. This may sound strange to some, because no one who believes in unconditional election to salvation will express these things in this way. 2 Thessalonians 2:13-14 is usually mentioned in regard to this discussion, but very briefly. It is often mentioned to show that the choice took place in eternity past before creation. In reality the verses say exactly the opposite. "From the beginning" is not the same as "before he foundation of the earth." There is a difference between "from" and "before."

The Timing of the Choice is "from the beginning." The timing in Ephesians 1:4 is "before the foundation of the world." The two statements are not the same. Another timing statement is found in John 1:1, "In the beginning." So here are three statements. "Before the foundation" equals *before creation*. "In the beginning" equals *at the time of creation*. From the beginning equals *sometime after the creation* or *starting at creation*. It's that simple. So, at the least, the timing of 2 Thessalonians 2:13-14 is *sometime after creation*. This choice to salvation took place in *time*, not eternity past!

However, the phrase "from the beginning" doesn't always refer to creation. In 1 John 1:1 it refers to the beginning of the life of Christ: "That which was *from the beginning*, which we have heard, which we have seen with our eyes, which we have looked upon, and our hands have handled, of the Word of life." In Acts 26:4-5, Paul uses the phrase to refer to the beginning of his productive life in the Jews religion. John 6:64 applies the phrase to the beginning of Christ's ministry. The same is true of John 15:27. "From the beginning" is a general phrase that could refer to any ongoing activity from any designated starting point.

So then, what was "the beginning" point for the Thessalonian Christians? There is another possible meaning of the phrase "from the beginning." Philippians 4:15

expresses it as "in the beginning *of the gospel.*" The phrase means "when the gospel first came to you." After that it would be expressed as "from the beginning of the gospel." The phrase, "From the beginning," clearly carries the same meaning in the context of 2 Thessalonians 2:13-14. This is verified by the fact that Paul connects it with their calling by the gospel in verse 14 and the other references to sanctification and belief. So, "from the beginning" refers to the time they heard the Gospel and the call of God through it. These things will be discussed more below. Regardless of the specific time, God chose us to salvation in *time*, not eternity past, before the creation.

God made the choice through means. That is, there was a method to how God chose them to salvation. The choosing is said to be "*through* sanctification...and belief..." The term *through* is defined by Webster: "By means of; by the agency of; noting instrumentality." [82] So the meaning of 2 Thessalonians 2:13 can be paraphrased as, "God hath ... chosen you ... *by means of* sanctification ... and belief." An example of this use of the term is found in John 17:17, "Sanctify them through thy truth: thy word is truth." How are we sanctified? It is "through" or "by means of" His truth. 1 Peter 1:2 says the same thing: "Elect ... through sanctification of the Spirit." So, God *chose us by sanctifying us* with the Spirit. This is the plain statement of God almighty, who works all things according to the good pleasure of His will. It was the good pleasure of His will to choose us to salvation *in time* not in eternity past and *by means of* sanctification and belief of the truth.

When were we sanctified by the Spirit? The first use of "sanctify" in the Bible is Exodus 13:2, where the Lord told

Israel to sanctify the firstborn to Him. Every Biblical use of the word in all its forms refers to something that is being done in time, not eternity. It never refers to eternity. You were sanctified by the Spirit when you got saved. This did not happen in eternity past. It happened during your life time. God chose you through sanctifying you by the Spirit. So you were elected to salvation in time, not eternity past.

To confirm this, there is another method by which God chose us. It is "through ... belief of the truth." So, our faith itself became the vehicle by which God chose us. Belief certainly took place in time and at the same time that we were sanctified. It did not take place in eternity past.

God calls the sinner to salvation by the gospel. "Whereunto he called you by our gospel, to the obtaining of the glory of our Lord Jesus Christ" (2 Thess. 2:14). "Whereunto" refers to the salvation of verse 13. The "call" of a sinner to salvation does not come through some inner compulsion or conviction. It comes through the gospel. The Holy Spirit convinces sinners through the Word of God. It can be added that the drawing of the sinner to come to Christ (John 6:44) is done through the Word of God, also. John 6:45 says, "It is written in the prophets, And they shall be all taught of God. Every man therefore that hath heard, and hath learned of the Father, cometh unto me." What do they hear? Do they hear some voice from heaven or a voice whispering in their ear? Or, do they hear the Word of God. Jesus said, "He that *heareth my word*, and believeth on him that sent me, hath everlasting life" (John 5:24). Those who hear the Word and believe are those who have "heard, and learned of the Father." Specifically, it is the gospel they hear (1 Cor. 15:1-4). The call of God and the drawing of the Spirit come through hearing the Word of God. This is especially important because "faith cometh by hearing, and hearing by the word of God" (Rom. 10:17). Faith (belief-verse 13) comes after hearing the gospel. Since faith is connected with the means by which God chooses, this also proves that election to salvation takes place in time, not eternity.

One important ingredient regarding predestination and election is foreknowledge. Rom. 8:28 says, "For whom he did foreknow, he also did predestinate ..." and 1 Peter 1:2 says, "Elect according to the foreknowledge of God the Father." Clearly foreknowledge is part of the process. However, a Calvinistic view would deny that foreknowledge has anything to do with it. The 1689 Baptist Confession, Chapter Three, Of God's Decree, paragraphs one through three, says:

> God hath decreed in himself, from all eternity, by the most wise and holy counsel of His own will, freely and unchangeably, all things, whatsoever comes to pass ... yet hath He not decreed anything, *because He foresaw it as future* ... By the decree of God, for the manifestation of His glory, some men and angels are predestinated, or foreordained to eternal life through Jesus Christ, to the praise of His glorious grace; others being left to act in their sin to their just condemnation, to the praise of His glorious justice. (Emphasis added.) [83]

Regardless of the opinions of men, God's Word says otherwise. The Greek word translated foreknowledge is the word from which we get the English word *prognosis*, which is an *educated prediction of the future condition* of a medical patient. It has to do with prior knowledge. Acts 2:23 uses this word and contrasts it with foreordination and the "determinate counsel" of God. In the death of Christ, both foreordination and foreknowledge were involved and both specifically and separately mentioned, indicating they are not the same.

These verses do not explicitly state what God foreknew. He certainly knew everything about each of us and our lives. However, there is something special and specific about this foreknowledge that makes it significant enough to mention in this context. *Vine's Expository Dictionary of Old and New Testament Words* says this:

> Prognosis (G4268), "a foreknowledge" ... is used only of divine "foreknowledge," Act 2:23; 1Pe 1:2. "Foreknowledge" is one aspect of omniscience; it is implied in God's warnings, promises and predictions. See Act 15:18. God's "foreknowledge" involves His electing grace, but this does not preclude human will. He "foreknows" the exercise of faith which brings salvation. The apostle Paul stresses especially the actual purposes of God rather than the ground of the purposes, see, e.g., Gal 1:16; Eph 1:5, Eph 1:11. The divine counsels will ever be unthwartable. [84]

Closely akin to *prognosis* is the Greek word *proginōsko*, which literally means "to know beforehand. The word *proginōsko* is translated with this meaning every time it's used in the New Testament except once. It is translated as "foreordained" in 1 Peter 1:20, "Forasmuch as ye know that ye were not redeemed with corruptible things, ... But with the precious blood of Christ ... Who verily was *foreordained* before the foundation of the world, but was manifest in these last times for you..." (1 Peter 1:18-20). The word is used in reference to Christ's death. It is never used in the sense of foreordained any other time. Acts 4:23 makes it clear that Christ's death was not only foreknown by God, it was also determined beforehand and foreordained, the KJV translators rendered it "foreordained" for this reason. The Bible never states that the salvation of specific individuals was foreordained or determined before the foundation of the earth.

Conclusion

No doubt, it is very apparent that I am not a Calvinist. I believe very strongly in the grace of God, but not like those who believe in the Calvinistic version of "the doctrines of Grace." My faith is stronger than theirs, because I believe His grace has been offered to all and can be experienced by all. However, I am certainly not an Armenian either! Armenians have a much weaker view of God's grace, believing that Christians can lose the salvation God so graciously gave them. They believe we are saved by grace through faith, but we must be obedient to God if we are to keep our salvation. As important as obedience is, it is not required to keep your salvation any more than it is required to obtain your salvation. The grace of God is as necessary and effective after we get saved as before. For centuries there has been a false dichotomy drawn between Calvinism and Armenianism. If you are not a Calvinist, you must be an Armenian. This is a false dichotomy. I try to be a Bible believer, no matter whose doctrine the Scriptures contradict. In this case, my view of the grace of God is much stronger than those who say they believe in the "doctrines of grace." In their view God only has enough grace to give salvation to a select *few*, while deliberately leaving the great majority of people to go to Hell. Grace that leads to salvation is not genuinely offered to them. On the other hand, I believe God's grace is genuinely offered to everyone and that anyone can come to God through Christ by the grace of God. Our God sincerely wishes every person to come to the knowledge of the truth and be saved. This is the true doctrine of grace.

    What shall we say then? Many theologians and thinkers and students of the Bible see in the Scriptures what they call Sovereign Grace or the doctrines of grace or Calvinism, that, before creation, God unconditionally chose certain individuals throughout history to be saved and chose to allow all others to die in their sins and go to hell. On the other hand, many of them also clearly see that the Bible depicts and treats people as if they have free will and can choose good over evil. They all know that the gospel call goes to all, whether elect or not, and it is preached that "whosoever will" may come. This clearly gives the impression that a free and equal opportunity for salvation is offered to everyone. They say, "It is a mystery." They cannot see how free will and their view of election could both be true, but many of them believe both. I have heard it explained something like this: Free will and unconditional election are like the rails of railroad tracks. They run parallel and seem to come together in the far distance. Election and free will are parallel truths and we do not see how they reconcile, but they do reconcile and someday we will understand it. Until then it is a mystery. In reality, the railroad tracks *never* come together and the ideas of unconditional election and total inability *cannot* be reconciled with free will. However, there are others who openly reject free will. I believe we can understand the truth about this so-called "mystery" right now, if we accept and believe the plain statements of Scripture.

Ephesians 1:4 is a profound and deep statement of truth. However, election is not a hidden mystery. It can be understood by believing precisely what we read in the word of God. In Ephesians 1:4, before the foundation of the world, God chose all who would be in Christ to ultimately be made morally holy and blameless. To that end He predestinated them to the adoption of children. In the past, He saved our souls and gave a new birth to our spirits. In the future, we are predestined to have new bodies and we will be completely sinless. He will save us from the very presence of sin in our lives. In this way, we will finally be confirmed in complete holiness and love before God. This is the plan and the assurance for the final destiny of all believers. The same truths are taught in Romans 8:23-30.

The doctrine of unconditional election flatly and forthrightly contradicts some cardinal truths of Scripture. God loved every individual in the world to the point that He sent His only begotten Son to die for them and pay the penalty of their sins. He loved and died for everyone.

Calvinism teaches that Christ only died for the elect. This is a serious contradiction. It is God's desire that everyone gets saved and comes to the knowledge of the truth. Unconditional election teaches that God only wants a few to get saved. In fact, the Scriptures teach that God is not willing that any perish (2 Pet. 3:9). Yet unconditional election teaches that God's plan determines that only a part of mankind will be saved and the rest will perish. Finally, unconditional election makes God a respecter of persons in judgment. Those persons may be sinners and God's respect may be unconditional, but nevertheless He shows favoritism in judgment toward a few chosen ones. The Scriptures teach that God's judgment is consistent for all. He has offered a way out of eternal punishment to all through the death and resurrection of Christ. He has declared that whosoever will, may believe and be saved. Those who won't shall perish. This judgment is applied without partiality or favoritism.

God does choose us to salvation (2 Thess. 2:13-14; 1 Peter 1:2). This choice is made in time, "from the beginning," which means sometime starting with the beginning of the gospel. Therefore, the choice to salvation was *not* made *before* the foundation of the world. The timing is further defined as being when we were sanctified by the Spirit and when we believed the gospel. This definition places the time God chose us at the same time we got saved. Sanctification of the Spirit and belief became the means by which God chose us. The choice was also according to God's foreknowledge.

The Bible tells us, "Hold fast the *form* of sound words, which thou hast heard of me, in faith and love which is in Christ Jesus" (2 Tim. 1:13). There are many words that have been written and spoken on the topic of unconditional election. Many of them have a strong flavor of human logic and philosophy applied to the Scriptures. When I was in college, during one class, a philosophy professor started with a Calvinistic view of the Sovereignty of God (he did not prove this view by Scripture) and built a complete Calvinistic structure based entirely on logic, not Scripture. So, words are piled upon words and volumes are written to the point where God's truth is complicated beyond any recognition. However, the words that count are not the words of John Calvin or the Reformers or the 1689 Baptist Confession or any professor or any pastor or any other commentator, including me. The only words that count are the words of Scripture. These are the form of sound words, to which Paul referred.

There is simplicity in Christ (2 Cor. 11:1-3). When we listen to His words in the Bible and judge the words of men by His words, many things become clear. This is what I have tried to do here. In Acts 17:11, God commends the Bereans because, when Paul taught them, they "received the word with all readiness of mind, and searched the scriptures daily, whether those things were so." Steve Jones, a former Calvinist, wrote a paper challenging the major points of Calvinism. In his concluding remarks he agrees:

> The average Calvinist may be amazed at just how weak his system is when scrutinized in the light of revealed truth. May our brethren see fit to adopt a Berean spirit (Acts 17:11) and honestly rethink their Calvinism. We would urge

them to, for a time, lay aside the commentaries of Calvin and Gill, the theology of Warfield and Hodge. With an open Bible and mind, may they take a second look at the so-called "doctrines of grace" to see if they truly are the doctrines of Christ.[85]

About the Author

Dr. Steve Combs is a Baptist minister. He spent his early years in Kentucky, Virginia, and finally Ohio. He was not raised in a Christian home. He had some Christian influence from his grandmother, but that had little effect on him. Due to discussions with a Baptist preacher and a Sunday School teacher, who visited his home, he began to read the Bible. The Word of God had its effect. He came under strong conviction of his sins. A friend invited him to a nearby church during revival meetings. As a result, he received Christ as his Savior.

Since then there have been major transformations to his life. God called him to preach and enabled a backward shy individual suffering from an inferiority complex to stand before crowds and confidently proclaim the Word of God. God gave him a business background as a CPA and put him in several ministry positions. He has served as a Bible Institute teacher, a youth pastor, and a senior pastor. He holds a Doctor of Theology from Covington Theological Seminary.

Currently Steve Combs is Assistant Director and a Global Translation Advisor for Bearing Precious Seed Global/ Global Bible Translators, www.bpsglobal.com. BPS Global starts and assists Bible translation projects around the world.

He is married and has four married children.

End Notes

[1] "International Standard Bible Encyclopedia." Ed. James Orr, John Nuelsen, Edgar Mullins, Morris Evans, and Melvin Grove Kyle. *E-Sword*. Rick Meyers. Version 10.2.1. Franklin, Tn.: 2013. Downloaded computer software.

[2] Hindson, Edward and Woodrow, Michael. "KJV Bible Commentary." *Libronix Digital Library System*. System 1.0c. Oak Harbor, WA: Libronix Corporation, copyright 2000-2001. CD ROM.

[3] International

[4] Webster, Noah. "Webster's Dictionary of American English." 1828 edition. *E-Sword*. Rick Meyers. Version 10.2.1. Franklin, Tn.: 2013. Downloaded computer software.

[5] Easton, M. G. "Easton's Bible Dictionary." *E-Sword*. Rick Meyers. Version 10.2.1. Franklin, Tn.: 2013. Downloaded computer software.

[6] Wiliams, Armstrong. *Why the Media Wants to Destroy Trump*. Published by Dennis Michael Lynch on Facebook, Oct. 10, 2016. Accessed Nov. 2016

[7] These statistics come from Wycliffe Bible Translators as of 2015

[8] Vine, W.E. "Vine's Complete Expository Dictionary of New Testament Words." *E-Sword*. Rick Meyers. Version 10.2.1.

Franklin, Tn.: 2013. Downloaded computer software.

[9] Webster

[10] Webster

[11] Vine's NT

[12] Thayer

[13] Webster

[14] Thayer

[15] Wikipedia http://en.wikipedia.org/wiki/John_Gill_(theologian) 3/6/2015. http://en.wikipedia.org/wiki/Crusades 3/20/2015.

[16] Gill, John. "John Gill's Exposition of the Entire Bible." *E-Sword*. Rick Meyers. Version 10.2.1. Franklin, Tn.: 2013. Downloaded computer software.

[17] Thayer

[18] Vine's NT

[19] Vine's NT

[20] Vine's NT

[21] Bridges, Jerry. *The Pursuit of Holiness.* Colorado Springs: Navpress, 1978. Print. 73

[22] Bridges

[23] Webster

[24] Bridges

[25] Bridges

[26] Bridges

[27] Bridges

[28] Pentecost, J. Dwight. *Things to Come.* Grand Rapids: Zondervan, 1958. Print.

[29] Thayer

[30] Larkin, Clarence. *Dispensational Truth.* Glenside, PA.: Rev. Clarence Larkin Est., 1920. Print. 150-151.

[31] MacDonald, William and Farstad, Art. "Believers Bible Commentary." *Libronix Digital Library System.* System 1.0c. Oak Harbor, WA: Libronix Corporation, copyright 2000-2001. CD-ROM.

[32] Hindson

[33] Webster

[34] Brown-Driver-Briggs Hebrew Definitions. *E-Sword*. Rick Meyers. Version 10.2.1. Franklin, Tn.: 2013. Downloaded computer software.

[35] Jameson, Robert; Fausett, A. R.; and Brown, David. "Jameson, Fausett, and Brown Commentary." *E-Sword*. Rick Meyers. Version 10.2.1. Franklin, Tn.: 2013. Downloaded computer software.

[36] Wikipedia

[37] "Expositor's Bible Commentary." Ed. William Nicholl. *E-Sword*. Rick Meyers. Version 10.2.1. Franklin, Tn.: 2013. Downloaded computer software.

[38] Johnson, Barton. "Peoples New Testament." *E-Sword*. Rick Meyers. Version 10.2.1. Franklin, Tn.: 2013. Downloaded computer software.

[39] Halley, Henry H. *Halley's Bible Handbook.* Grand Rapids: Zondervan, 1965. Print.

[40] Ryrie Balancing

[41] Ryrie, Charles C. *Balancing the Christian Life*. Chicago: Moody Press, 1969. Print.

[42] Mills, Eddie. Facebook page post. August 28, 2016. Web. Accessed August 30, 2016.

[43] Webster

[44] Thayer

[45] Webster

[46] Webster

[47] Webster

[48] Webster

[49] Webster

[50] Webster

[51] Webster

[52] MacDonald

[53] MacDonald

[54] Peoples

⁵⁵ Ryrie

⁵⁶ Webster/Thayer

⁵⁷ Webster

⁵⁸ *Global Research: IMB*. International Mission Board. 2014. Web. 7 October 2014.

⁵⁹ International Bible Encyclopedia

⁶⁰ Thayer

⁶¹ Newell, William. "Romans Verse by Verse." Bible *Analyzer 4*. Timothy Morton. Version 4.9.2.10. Morton Publications. Downloaded computer software.

⁴⁸ Erickson, Millard J. <u>Christian Theology 2ⁿᵈ Edition.</u> (Grand Rapids: Baker Academic, 2005) 929.

₄₉ *VOR*. "1689 London Baptist Confession." Vor.org. 1996. Web. 28 March 2016.

⁵⁰ Calvin, John. <u>Institutes of the Christian Religion</u>, Book 3 Ch. 21. 1559. E-Sword. Rick Meyers. Version 10.2.1. Franklin, Tn.: 2013. Downloaded computer software.

⁵¹ Erickson, 929

66 *VOR.*

67 Ante-Nicene Fathers. Vol. 1. *E-Sword*. Rick Meyers. Version 10.2.1. Franklin, Tn.: 2013. Downloaded computer software.

68 Ante-Nicene Fathers. Vol. 1.

69 Ante-Nicene Fathers. Vol. 1.

70 Ante-Nicene Fathers. Vol. 1.

71 Ante-Nicene Fathers. Vol. 3. *E-Sword*. Rick Meyers. Version 10.2.1. Franklin, Tn.: 2013. Downloaded computer software.

72 Ante-Nicene Fathers. Vol. 5. *E-Sword*. Rick Meyers. Version 10.2.1. Franklin, Tn.: 2013. Downloaded computer software.

73 Vine's

74 Jones, Steve. Calvinism Critiqued by a Former Calvinist. Auburn University. Open House Church Articles. Web. June 11, 2015.

75 Jamieson, Faussett, and Brown

[76] Thayer

[77] Thayer

[78] Thayer

[79] Pappas, John. <u>Bible Greek Basic Grammar of the New Testament</u>. John Pappas: http://biblegreekvpod.com/File/Bible_Greek_vpod.pdf. 2008. Web Book, 65.

[80] Thayer

[81] Thayer

[82] Webster

[83] VOR. 1689 Baptist Confession

[84] Vine's

[85] Jones, Steve

www.ingramcontent.com/pod-product-compliance
Lightning Source LLC
Chambersburg PA
CBHW071329190426
43193CB00041B/1037